This book provides excellent insight, by a prominent scientist, into the socio-technical and human quality aspects of information and communication technology.

Gavriel Salvendy, *Professor of Industrial Engineering at Purdue University and Chair Professor and Head of the Department of Industrial Engineering at Tsinghua University, Beijing, P.R. of China*
http://www.iems.ucf.edu/salvendy/

More than fifty years of sustained empirical research on the psychosocial and organizational consequences of information and communication technologies is Gunilla Bradley's contribution to understanding how computerization has transformed the world, politics and economy, the work setting, and our private lives. Today we find ourselves in an environment where computer, information, and media technologies have become indispensable and have converged to confound and, indeed, dissolve former distinctions between our public, work, and private lives. Yet, as much as there is the negative to this convergence, there is equally also the positive. It is with the wisdom gained from her decades of research and with great empathy and optimism for the human condition that Gunilla Bradley reflects on the choices before us. She asks us to evaluate the life conditions that we want, the characteristics of a good work environment and technologies that help us attain our goals, and properties of our social structures, norms, and values systems that promote a positive climate for our world and societies that have been transformed by computerization.

Alice Robbin, *Indiana University Bloomington, USA*

At times an introduction to concepts, at others a plea for action, this little book of wisdom is also a cross between an autobiography and a diary – it brings together in one place the latest in a lifetime of work. Its 100 or so pages really show how policy, people and practices all need to be brought together when co-creating digital technologies. Look out especially for Gunilla Bradley's manifestos!

Diane Whitehouse, *Chair – ICT and Society Technical Committee, International Federation for Information Processing*

T0383739

The Good ICT Society

What is *quality of life* in a society that has embraced information and communication technology (ICT)? What is *wisdom* in this kind of society? And what things are helping or hindering us from having both wisdom and a good quality of life in ICT societies?

Taking the reader through a quick analysis of the current social and psychological changes in the Information and Communication Society, Bradley challenges us to avoid becoming victims of technology – whether we are professionals, policymakers, parents, or citizens. Indeed, she introduces a theoretical model based on four decades' worth of research to help the reader to understand this complex technological world. In addition to focusing the reader's attention on *convergence and acceleration*, this model describes the interplay between technology, societal structure, organizational design, and human roles, thus leading to what Bradley describes as a *Good ICT Society*.

Emphasizing the necessity of a co-operative parallel between the automation and humanization of society, this innovative volume will be of interest to undergraduate and postgraduate students and postdoctoral researchers interested in the subjects such as Information and Communication Technology and Social Change, Psychology and Sociology, Computer Technology, and Media Technology.

Gunilla Bradley is Professor Emerita in Informatics at Royal Institute of Technology (KTH) – School of ICT in Stockholm. GB is originally a psychologist and has a broad background in the social and behavioral sciences. Her research concerns the interplay between Information and Communication Technology (ICT), Human Beings, and Society – Social Informatics. Her cross disciplinary research groups were first hosted by Stockholm University for twenty years. She has then been a visiting professor at Stanford University two years and professor of Technology and Social Change at the Royal Institute of Technology. From 1997–2001 she served as professor in Informatics at Umeå University and Mid Sweden University. In 1997 she received the prestigious Namur Award from IFIP for her pioneering research to increase the social awareness of the impact of ICT. Gunilla has authored thirteen books and contributed extensively in international scientific journals and the popular science press. Her latest book *Social and Community Informatics – Humans on the Net* (Routledge 2006) is widely used in both ICT related disciplines and in the social sciences. In 2008 Gunilla was invited as guest professor in Salzburg. She initiated and chaired the annual IADIS conference on "ICT, Society and Humans" for some years. In 2010 she was honored by a "Fest Symposium" at Linnaeus University in Sweden and a "Festschrift" (Eds. Haftor & Mirijamdotter, 2011). More than 60 distinguished researchers from all continents of the world contributed with chapters. Gunilla is currently writing the book *The Good Information and Communication Society – From Theory to Action* (Routledge).

Routledge Research in Information Technology and Society

For a full list of titles in this series, please visit https://www.routledge.com/Routledge-Research-in-Information-Technology-and-Society/book-series/SE0448

The Good ICT Society
From Theory to Actions

Gunilla Bradley

Routledge
Taylor & Francis Group

LONDON AND NEW YORK

First published 2017 by Routledge

2 Park Square, Milton Park, Abingdon, Oxfordshire OX14 4RN
52 Vanderbilt Avenue, New York, NY 10017

Routledge is an imprint of the Taylor & Francis Group, an informa business

First issued in paperback 2019

Copyright © 2017 Gunilla Bradley

The right of Gunilla Bradley to be identified as author of this work
has been asserted by her in accordance with sections 77 and 78 of the
Copyright, Designs and Patents Act 1988.

All rights reserved. No part of this book may be reprinted or reproduced
or utilised in any form or by any electronic, mechanical, or other means,
now known or hereafter invented, including photocopying and recording,
or in any information storage or retrieval system, without permission in
writing from the publishers.

Notice:
Product or corporate names may be trademarks or registered trademarks,
and are used only for identification and explanation without intent to
infringe.

British Library Cataloguing-in-Publication Data
A catalogue record for this book is available from the British Library

Library of Congress Cataloging-in-Publication Data
A catalog record for this book has been requested

ISBN: 978-1-138-29429-5 (hbk)
ISBN: 978-0-367-88650-9 (pbk)

Typeset in Times New Roman
by Apex CoVantage, LLC

To Lydia, Nadja, Cate

Contents

Figures

Preface

What is *quality of life* in a society that has embraced information and communication technology (ICT)? What is *wisdom* in this kind of society? And what things are helping or hindering us from having both wisdom and a good quality of life in ICT societies?

Think of how our roles at work, in private, and as citizens overlap. Working from home and "homing" from work defines our modern lifestyle. We are all empowered by mobile technology, from smart phones to smart cars. We have to avoid becoming victims of technology, whether we are professionals, policymakers, parents, citizens, or all of the above.

We can understand the complex world we are entering through a simple theoretical model based on my research over the past four decades. *Convergence and acceleration* are the main processes in the model, describing the interplay between technology, societal structure, organizational design, and human roles in society. This model and my research on both risks and opportunities in the 21st century ICT society inform what I describe as a *Good ICT Society*. I also call for *actions* that we need for a good and sustainable society.

The core message in my book is that the automation and humanization of society should go hand in hand. Today we focus too much on technology development and too little on human development in a technological world. We can have both.

The book takes the reader from a quick analysis of the current social and psychological changes in the ICT society to actions towards a good and sustainable ICT society. This road is supported by the convergence theory I have developed over the course of my career – an illustrative model for understanding the ICT society and for finding ways for actions and guidelines that are needed in a complex society.

I share voices from around the world to show the deep impact of ICT on human beings and their perception of what is of value in life. They express enthusiasm, as well as frustrations and worries.

One *purpose* of the book is to provide a set of guidelines, what I am thinking of as my manifesto. A short book is required to get my message across: there are too many thick books in the world, and the time to read is limited and the time to act is now. Speed is of the essence.

My experience is unique: my background in psychology, joined with more than 40 years of research in this field, has led to empirical results from four main historical periods of computerization (digitalization). I also have a unique view, with international comparative research paired with my main focus on Sweden, an early adopter of computers, with politics in between the socialism and capitalism. Cross-disciplinary research describes my own academic background and my work with my research colleagues.

I bring my experience to bear on this book and hope to deliver it as soon as possible, in a world where information and communication technology interacts with and drives everything at an increasing rate, from war and conflicts to rethinking of human roles, behavior, values, gender equality, and economic theory and practice.

The chapter titles of the book can serve as a quick view and hopefully an appetizer!

- Visions of a Way Forward
- In Search of Quality of Life and Wisdom in the ICT society
- The Convergence Model: A Path to the Golden Rule
- Towards Peace on Earth
- Voices from around the World on Quality of Life and Well-being in the ICT Society
- The Good ICT Society
- Tree of Action

Who do I want to reach? In fact, each one of you!

One group is academics at the beginning of their studies in ICT-related disciplines; I have got many comments from colleagues in that direction, that students need a broader societal perspective before they specialize into the ever-growing sub-disciplines of ICT. Another group of academics are behavioral scientists and other social scientists that have to understand the life of persons in the ICT society. Still another group is teachers in obligatory school, physicians, parents, and policy makers.

The main content is of global interest and is asked for in most continents, due to the adoption and use of ICT worldwide. I have been an active member in several international associations and participant in many conferences related to information and communication technology.

These conferences (annual and biannual), universities, and technical universities are "home" to researchers and students who would be interested in this book.

My contribution is that I present a broad cross-disciplinary theoretical perspective (convergence theory) that helps to understand the present-day society and ongoing processes, and from there I also depict actions that should or could be taken on various levels in society, including by us as individual human beings, to reach what I call the Good ICT Society. A special chapter is devoted to analyzing what a good and sustainable society is. My purpose is that this little book – and it is a small book – could inspire and encourage a broader audience outside the academic world and increase an awareness and involvement that is necessary to avoid / prevent big clashes that society might face in the near future with increasing ICT.

There are many persons I would like to thank for inspiration, encouragement, and support during the process of creating my book. Hence I have devoted a special section with acknowledgements.

Dear Reader, I would love to have comments and any input from you on my book. Please send mail to gbradley@kth.se, with subject line: "Good ICT society".

Gunilla Bradley
Stockholm, 2016

1 Visions of a way forward

1.1 Introduction

Wisdom is a big word. It has often been used to talk about data included in informatics and computer science as part of a string of other words: information, knowledge, wisdom (Ackoff, 1989).

Colleagues have warned me against using such a big word; others have expressed enthusiasm, saying that wisdom is what we need today. Still others have asked me about the process, about how to craft wisdom. To answer these questions, I have been trying to draw from my research and experiences over the years, bringing together what is available in the research world, and interviewing people who have been researching the field of information and communications technology (ICT) and social and societal change. This little book is a kind of synthesis, a trial to bring together my research experiences – theoretical, empirical, and visionary – ending up in a manifesto. Out of my 12 earlier books, the last few have been big bricks, and it is time to be short!

I would like to start with some guiding principles and statements, at the same time as I sum up what I want you, my reader, to take away from this text (Figure 1.1).

What do I mean by wisdom? There are many possible definitions:

> The quality of having experience, knowledge, and good judgment . . . The soundness of an action or decision with regard to the application of experience, knowledge, and good judgment. . . . The body of knowledge and principles that develops within a specified society or period.
>
> (Oxford Dictionaries)

Figure 1.1 Art and music are the only world languages
Source: (Åke Hassbjer, 2014)

> Wisdom involves an understanding of people, objects, and situations. It often requires control of one's emotional reactions so that the universal principle of reason determines one's action. Wisdom is seen as a disposition to find the truth coupled with an optimum judgement as to what actions should be taken.
>
> (Wikipedia)

Wisdom might be viewed from various perspectives: philosophical, psychological, sociological, and pedagogical. From these various perspectives, I think that academia should change its focus from solely seeking knowledge to the promotion of wisdom. We need to increase our competence to understand what is of value in life, for oneself, the other and the society as a whole. New knowledge and technological development in general are empowering human beings to take actions within most fields; however, the actions need to be governed and accompanied by wisdom. There is otherwise a high risk of human suffering instead of human well-being. Wisdom is the use of knowledge to achieve desirable goals for humankind.

I think that in order to become wise, one needs to start by asking questions. What are the key questions in the field of ICT society and human beings? What issues need to be taken care of most urgently? Let's start by examining general phenomena at a societal level (something I will examine more carefully in section 6.2, "From an information society for all to quality of life for all"). This brings me back to a quote from my book from 1977, *Computer Technology, Work Life and Communication*:

> The next generation will grow up in a computer society and already in school use computers. It will probably view the computer as a natural and independent tool. We are at the same time experiencing a period of transition in democracy at work and society, which naturally leads forward to that people are raising a couple of questions. This is positive

prerequisite for a research that is focusing issues of relevance for the long term societal development.

(Bradley, 1977, p. 57)

Almost four decades ago, I tried to pinpoint these key issues in my book *Professional Roles and Life Environment* (1979) and at a conference held in Montreal in 1981 on the quality of working life. Today, these issues continue to remain at the nexus of the future of ICT and society.

* *The data processing technology arms race*
* *Energy questions and data processing questions*
* *The allocation questions*
* *Home computer revolution*
* *Aspects of equality*

What was the situation in the 1970s and 1980s, and what's new today? Concerning the *the data processing technology arms race*, the competition at the time focused on technology, and no side-effects were identified that could be connected to weapons. Concerning *energy questions and data processing questions*, computer power was at the time initially perceived as an industry with low energy requirements. Concerning *the allocation questions*, I would say that this is still a central issue. Concerning *home computer revolution*, personal computers (PCs) had appeared and were perceived as "the" new home tool.

Aspects of equality: Three decades ago, people had not yet thought about the balance between cultures, regarding male-female audiences, religion, ethnicity, and so forth. In 1996, the first use of the phrase "digital divide" began a discussion about the split between those with and without computers.

In the year 2017 these issues are still a deep concern; however, some of them have changed their character and focus, so let's look at some of these changes.

The data processing technology arms race in 1979 was understood in the context of the Cold War between the former Soviet Union and Western countries. Nuclear weapons together with computer power were perceived as a new increased risk for the world and as the start of a new kind of war. Today this concern has shifted to the risk of *cyber-attacks and a cyber-war*, together with the growing phenomenon of *surveillance*. I will discuss this in detail in Chapter 4 on "Toward Peace on Earth".

When it comes to *energy questions and data processing questions*, ICT today plays an important role as a tool to minimize the use of energy resources, for example, in homes and buildings. But at the end of its life, electronics waste or e-waste requires energy to process and recycle, and researchers are working a lot to minimize the "costs" in that process.

The *allocation or distribution issue* is still a key question. Accumulation of capital and other resources (human and material) is speeded up by ICT. Distribution of resources could also be facilitated by ICT.

The home computer revolution that was anticipated in the late 1970s has come to pass – and passed, in a way. The converging technologies within ICT and the increasing use of mobile smart phones have been strong drivers behind the process of converging human roles at home, at work, and in society at large. I will examine this more carefully in Chapter 2, looking at how humans have become totally dependent on ICT.

Finally *aspects on equality in general* are still fundamental. Most democracies try to address aspects of *equality between the sexes*, albeit slowly, using various strategies. But a quick view of the state of gender equality at the society level is depressing and shows that it is still a severe problem. There are very few women in leading positions worldwide – in technology, in politics, and associations/bodies that deal with peace and in general bodies that are extremely powerful in these areas.

"Risks and opportunities" in work life and at home is a classical way to describe key issues. I specified the main risks and opportunities in my book *Computers and the Psychosocial Work Environment* (1989 [1986 in Sweden]), and I mentioned *employment* and various aspects of *work content* and *working conditions*. The computerization of society began in working life; however, aspects such as *vulnerability* and *integrity* have moved over to become more valid in society as a whole due to cyber war risks and surveillance. Factors within the so-called psychosocial work environment are still sensitive to the use of ICT and for a long time also have concerned the life outside what we call work. We can talk about a *psychosocial life environment* – this is evident when reading and analyzing what people say and something I will examine in Chapter 5 on "Voices from around the world on quality of life and well-being".

I think that there are some fundamental and basic prerequisites to having a good quality of life. These require reflecting on technology and where it has taken us, as well as where we want to go now.

Let me also first make a position statement that ICT per se is a "beautiful technology" – with a high potential for the Good Society for All – an embryo for democracy, well-being, health, and quality of life for all.

1.2 Major goals in the ICT society

In the decades following my first forays into these issues, I examined policy and other issues that lay out the major goals in what I refer to as the ICT society. I can boil these down to 10 main goals for which I would advocate concern in the development, introduction, and use of ICT. These will be addressed again at the end of the book.

- *Human welfare* and *life quality for all*
- *Humanization*
- *E-cooperation and peace*
- *Integration and respect for diversity*
- *Democracy*
- *Autonomy*
- *Balance/harmony*
- *Sustainability*
- *The unforeseen*

ICT should contribute to the deepening and development of true human qualities and be used to provide time for people to develop themselves as human beings (humanization). Any type of e-conflict must be prevented (e-cooperation). ICT should contribute to enrichment of the social contact between people and should be used to prevent social isolation. ICT should facilitate integration and thereby also respect diversity. ICT should be used for deepening and broadening democracy. ICT should contribute to greater autonomy for the individual. Control or freedom is a classic issue. ICT should facilitate *information access for all* and support individual learning, but at the same time *prevent stress* and various kinds of overload. ICT should support the human and societal goal of sustainability – including the environment, economy, and human beings. ICT should be used for preparing for the unforeseen and preventing foreseen catastrophes, such as global warming. I addressed the issue of major goals for the ICT society at my Namur lecture (1997) and in my book *Humans on the Net* (2001), which was released the year Sweden chaired the EU.

The *first official statement* in the direction of my visions was the so-called Vilnius Declaration taken at the first World Information Technology Forum (WITFOR) in 2003. How can statements from WITFOR 2003 best be *transferred and adapted to the current technological development and the current world situation*? Fourteen years have passed since that event. I use this as a broader background to addressing what Good ICT Society for humans looks like (Chapter 6), which also is the main content in more action-oriented Chapter 7.

- bridging the digital *divide* between rich and poor in the world; urban and rural societies; men and women; and different generations;
- ensuring the *freedom of expression* enshrined in Article 19 of the Universal Declaration of Human Rights and other such instruments;
- reducing *poverty* through the use of education and information and communications technology;

- facilitating the *social integration* of excluded segments of societies;
- respecting linguistic and cultural *diversity*;
- fostering the creation of *public domains* with full respect of intellectual property rights (IPR);
- supporting communities in fighting *illiteracy*;
- encouraging *e-governance* and e-democracy initiatives;
- improving the *quality of life* through effective health service systems;
- protecting the local and global environment for *future generations*.

1.3 Effects on human beings

I think it is necessary to illustrate not only the effects on humans of ICT, but what a Good ICT Society might look like in the future. It can be directly related to my convergence model, which I describe in Chapter 3. In the middle of the model or "Round Trip Model" (since it was discussed over the years in many places in the world), there is a very helpful compass rose. A kind of Venn diagram is needed about ICT in human lives.

The most sensitive issues today, when it comes to effects on humans of ICT, are complex and multifaceted. Every aspect of these issues could be strengthened or weakened, depending on factors analyzed in the following chapters and conclusions in the final chapter on actions. Today, I am most concerned about the following issues: identity and self-perception in an ICT world; empathy; trust; dependence and addiction; gender balance; and empowerment. I want to highlight here briefly the importance of the last aspect of a Good ICT Society: empowerment. The paradox of empowerment in an ICT world is that people are empowered and therefore have new responsibilities at a global scale. This leads us to the question of *how* humans can become good global citizens.

What is it important to emphasize when it comes to the *main positive and negative effects on human beings of ICT*? While I will address this in the larger context of the convergence model in Chapter 2, I want to mention now that individuals are affected by ICT in many ways: their "life environments", "life roles", and through "globalization". The introduction of "virtual reality" will have impacts on these arenas and *add* a new sphere of ICT influence on human beings. Human beings can also influence these areas included the new virtual reality. Both interactions and convergences characterize the dynamics of the model. The way humans handle their situations can be either active or passive. Examples of *active reactions* are involvement, creative behavior, and protest. Examples of *passive reactions* are alienation, withdrawal, and certain psycho-physiological symptoms.

1.4 Voices from around the world

My voice is not the only one you will read in this book. I have taken published articles, books, and talks, as well as conversations with my academic colleagues and people in everyday life into account in coming to this point in time and in making my conclusions about a Good ICT Society. In my exploration of how people perceive ICT, I have heard both positive and negative views on ICT.

Most positive aspects or advantages?

The key positive issues perceived were: accessibility; the enabling, enriching and facilitating of life; the possibilities offered by speed; and, last but not least, the opportunities offered for the environment.

The dominant word regarding positive change was *access*. The people interviewed showed a clear enthusiasm about the new opportunity of having access, thereby mentioning human knowledge; family; friends; and strangers, even in foreign countries. Other aspects that people mentioned and which concerned the notion of access were finding a partner for work or love and companionship; getting access to institutions; and reaching financial information. Other areas mentioned were access to books and articles; news; entertainment; education; and health information.

Some emphasized and qualified the word "access" by referring to the *enabling, enriching, and facilitating of life*. Less often mentioned was "access independent of physical distance". Some people highlighted the great opportunity for *independence* offered by technologies – you do not need to ask other people for certain things.

More indirectly, the issue of *speed* was expressed by using such words as *fast, immediately, swiftly*, and *easy*.

Only one of the persons interviewed mentioned the positive potential for the *environment* due to the reduction in travelling.

Most negative aspects or disadvantages?

Most of the interviewees mentioned *a loss of important qualities in human beings, and the interaction between humans*. This seems to be the case in spite of all the former mentioned positive things. Here I list some key words and phrases from the interviews:

- A distance between human beings
- Decline on quality, reliability, and trustworthiness of content
- Identity problems
- Fraudsters

- Vulnerability of youngsters and of old people
- Difficulties of children to handle smart phones
- Addictiveness
- Negative influence of smart phones for the total life
- Hard for children
- Violence and children's behaviour
- Confusion between virtual and real world

The other group of responses concerned various aspects of *stress* due to the increase of diversity of goods, services, and information. These are the words used by the respondents:

- Too much time for making choices
- Exhausting and time-consuming
- Distracting
- Hard to focus on essentials
- Less time for silence, meditation, and deep interactions
- Loss of liberty due to the perceived pressure to react rapidly to emails

Do the words used by the respondents mirror the situation in Western cultures?

What does quality of life (or "a good life") mean for you and what contributes most to a good quality of life for you?

Some persons summarized in a *comprehensive* way and mentioned *several real aspects.* Let me exemplify with the words of one person: feeling secure; having a home, loved ones, family, friends; not fearing loss of basics, such as a stable home, food, and amenities for you and your family. Living in a society that is equal, democratic, and open, where all are treated with respect and have good living conditions.

Others focus on aspects of *freedom*: for example, being able to do what they want and when. Others mention some *specific issues* like: have a job; earn enough; be healthy; when a doctor's help is needed, receive it immediately; have access to the Internet and phone. Having a *good work-life balance* was often mentioned.

A few people mentioned some more *psychosocial and philosophical aspects*, such as:

- Continuously learning things and enjoying a proper balance and *enjoying all the senses* of our body.
- *Active engagement* in something that benefits others; opportunities for physical exercise and the enjoyment of nature; time for reflection.

- Not fearing to lose basic functions as a stable home, food, and amenities for you and your family. Living in a society that is *equal, democratic and open*, where all are treated with respect and have good living conditions.
- A sense of community; an interesting job that provides *contributions to the community* and the environment; a lifestyle with a low environmental impact.
- Family and friends are a given I assume: Talking and thinking about *"real" issues and trying to do something* about them, creative projects, engage with people – seeing art, theatre, etc., walking and wandering around.
- *Peace and freedom* are also assumed; easy access to intellectual and cultural richness, having numerous friends, *quietness and beauty* of nature.
- Trying to *spread happiness* and joy around which repays it tenfold.
- *Four factors that interact*: ecology, economy, politics, and culture.

Again I think that in general the main aspects that contribute to having a good life and quality of life concern very basic factors and it is important to reflect on where technology has taken us and where we want to go from now. This is also emphasized when we look at the factors (aspects) which are regarded as the most positive things related with ICT.

Questions about life in general, human life, and people's lives

Questions I have asked about life in general have led people to talk to me about a broader view of ICT, looking at risks and opportunities. Some of my sources focus on the opportunity for global business, global movements, and true democracy, which could be viewed as ways of expressing and describing *the Good ICT Society*. But a second group of voices you will hear from might describe *the Bad ICT Society:* these responses might be categorized as "top-down risks", for example, from governments monitoring their own people, or "bottom-up risks", for example, from subgroups of society organized in networks that eventually come to pose a threat – think about Daesh, for example, and its rise via the Internet. While you will read more in Chapter 5 on these multiple voices, I will discuss the Good ICT Society more in depth in Chapter 6, and address how we can move in the direction to reach that society, in Chapter 7.

1.5 The Good ICT Society and actions to reach that society

Again I would like to make the statement that ICT per se is a "beautiful technology" – with a high potential for the Good Society for All – an embryo for democracy, well-being, health, and quality of life for all. I have kept a similar sentence for two decades on my home page as a mini manifesto (Figure 1.2).

However, actions are needed urgently at all levels – international, national, regional, local, and personal – to make sure that these goals are realized. We as a global, regional, local society, and we as individuals, must find ways to create a Good and Sustainable ICT Society, with both short- and long-term perspectives. This, dear reader, is the goal of this book. I have been thinking and pondering and processing and identifying the most important things to do. In my mind, "Toward peace on Earth" (Chapter 4) and "The Good ICT Society" (Chapter 6) can be addressed through what I call a "Tree of Action" (Chapter 7). It is in this last chapter that I address tools, levels of actions, and stakeholders for getting to where we want to be in the future.

You will read these actions on how to achieve a good and sustainable society in my final chapter of this book. To give you a taste, I think we need to reflect on and act on:

> *World philosophy*, where "The Golden Rule" could be the unifying seed/cell and a world philosophy that focuses on "peace building".
>
> *Revision of economic theories* so they could match the present ICT society.
>
> *Politics* that build on common goals and livelihood, such as global warming and pandemics.
>
> *International Agreements and Statements such as . . .*
>
> *Education and learning.* These are powerful elements, and "preschool time" is fundamental for forming good global citizens. Examples will be mentioned in the later part of the book.
>
> *ICT.* Technology per se is a strong driver with quite wise new applications with wise guiding principles. . . .
>
> *Labor market.* Nordic Work life research from 1970s is a golden source . . .
>
> *The allocation issue* is crucial and generic . . . could take a new road at digitalization . . .
>
> *Distribution and balance*
>
> *Distribution of resources*
>
> *Global concerns.* We are all users of ICT.

These headlines give a hint of what components that could build a Good ICT Society (Figure 1.3). The road to a tree of action goes through the following chapters. Actions towards peace on earth will be addressed in Chapter 4.

This first chapter is a summing up of the content of this book. I also recommend the reader to explore some of the suggested Further Reading below and after some of the chapters to follow.

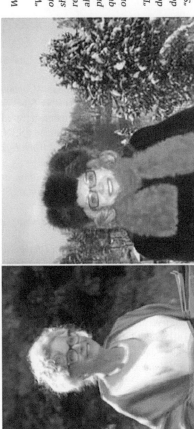

Welcome to my World!

"We have now a wholly new chance to explore the human side of societal change and take advantage of the technology to shape a good and balanced life. Let us use this opportunity for redesigning society towards peace, democracy and welfare for all ...those who will develop, introduce and use technology that promotes peace, a deepening of democracy, welfare and quality of life for all will be the winners" (Bradley in "Humans on the Net", 2001 p. 21)

"De som inför, utvecklar och använder IT för att fördjupa demokratin och för att skapa välfärd och livskvalitet - det är de som är de nya vinnarna" (intervju med Bradley i boken "Scener från ett arbetsliv", 2002 s. 113)

Figure 1.2 My homepage

Figure 1.3 At the age of two and four
Photo: Gunilla Bradley

Bibliography

Ackoff, R.L. (1989). From Data to Wisdom. *Journal of Applied Systems Analysis*, 16, 3–9.
Bradley, G. (1977). *Computer Technology, Work Life and Communication*. Report to the Swedish delegation for long term research (FRN). Stockholm: Liber.
Bradley, G. (1979). Professional Roles and Life Environment (Swedish title: *Yrkesroller och Livsmiljö*). Stockholm, SE: Wahlström, & Widstrand. ISBN: 91-46-13409-3.
Bradley, G. (1989). *Computers and the Psychosocial Work Environment*. London/ Philadelphia, UK/PA: Taylor & Francis.
Bradley, G. (ed.). (2001). *Humans on the Net: Information and Communication Technology (ICT) Work Organization and Human Beings*. Stockholm, SE: Prevent. ISBN: 91-7522-701-0.
Bradley, G.(2006). *Social and Community Informatics – Humans on the Net*. London/ New York: Routledge.
Bradley, G. (2015). TED Talk by Gunilla Bradley on *Change of Habits in the ICT Society*. http://tedxtalks.ted.com/video/Understanding-the-Change-of-Hab. *A TED seminar was held* in November 2014 in the city of Växjö at the Linnaeus University in Sweden, organized by Dr Miranda Kajtazi.
https://en.oxforddictionaries.com/definition/wisdom
https://en.wikipedia.org/wiki/Wisdom#Definitions
Khakhar, D. (ed.). (2003). *WITFOR 2003 White Book, Proceedings of IFIP World Information Technology Forum*. Laxenburg, Austria: IFIP Press.
WITFOR World IT Forum: Vilnius Declaration 2003, p. 2; see also Khakhar (2003).

2 In search of quality of life and wisdom in the ICT society

- Introduction
- Work life and private life
- Humans to robots
- Stress
- Communication between people
- Children
- Summing up
- Bibliography
- Appendix (Chapter 2)

2.1 Introduction

On a warm June day in 2015 I gave a keynote presentation at the International Society for Information Studies Summit in Vienna. The conference's many streams and tracks highlighted the multiple ways that technology, philosophy, and information interact with each other. I would have liked to have joined every session. For my part, I presented some "snap shots" from my research with colleagues over the years, but mainly from the past few years.

Since 1973, I have started up a number of research programs that have dealt with four main historical periods of computerization and ICT, from the mainframe period, with the use of batch processing systems, to the online period and use of display terminals, onward to micro-computerization with the appearance of microchips, and finally moved forward into the period of the Internet, where communication technologies have come to play a dominant role in the convergence of all technologies.

Think of all the industries impacted by communications technologies today, and you will be thinking of companies and industries I have studied: the national postal service, insurance, electronics, aircraft, banking, "high tech" in Silicon Valley, and even projects on the community level. I have scrutinized my own community and the village, Högsby, in the region of Småland, where I grew up, and did three years of voluntary work. This experience is described in depth in Chapter 6 in Bradley (2006) under the headline "Computers in the Bakery".

Being a researcher focused on "ICT, Organizational Change and Human Beings" was not easy. Power and computers are closely related. Computers were initially identified as a competitive tool in Sweden – a strategic focus for a small country which is dependent on international trade and export. Such criticism was not always popular. And yet, I called for critical analysis, referring to my research on both opportunities and risks when computers were being folded into work life and everyday life. However, when I ended the big projects by publishing my ideas a book, I was and still am eager to present my visions and possible actions on various levels.

My academic affiliation has been at several Swedish universities, with 20 years spent at Stockholm University. I spent two years at Stanford University in the USA. Over the last few years I have been doing my research at Kungliga Tekniska Högskolan (KTH), or the Royal Institute of Technology in Stockholm, Sweden. In the KTH and its School of ICT – where I made my academic home – are at the frontiers of high-tech research, and one of the two campuses is located right in the geographic middle of the Swedish IT and telecom industries.

Travelling from Sweden on that speaking trip to Vienna, I left from Arlanda International Airport just north of Stockholm. The walls of the airport are papered with huge photos. Perhaps you will come face to face with the King and Queen of Sweden as you are walking through the airport halls, or the internationally known Swedish pop group ABBA. On that particular trip, I came across these images (Figure 2.1).

Figure 2.1 Photos at Arlanda airport, Stockholm in 2015
Photo: Gunilla Bradley

"Welcome to the networked society", read one giant image, tagged with the mobile phone giant Ericsson's URL. Next, I was confronted with a wall-spanning image of the Stockholm city skyline, splashed with the text, "Mobile communication was born in Stockholm. Now it is transforming the world" – some bragging here.

Sweden can certainly be proud of its work in ICT. It can also boast about studying the impacts of ICT on our lives, starting with my own research on computerization in 1972. At the time, the focus was very strong on work life in Sweden, owing to the country's labor market organizations and the so called Swedish model, where there was a power balance between the employers and the employees/workers. But Swedes have the same challenges that people in the rest of the world do with balancing ICT in their work and private lives.

2.2 Work life and private life

Work life: network organizations

- Direct communication
- Barriers between ideas and execution disappear
- Power relocated
- Openness – borderless
- Multidimensional virtual culture
- Human competence is the currency
- Immediate distribution of information
- Network management and network competency
- Core workforce is decreasing
- Peripheral workforce is increasing (Temporary/agency employees; part-time staff; self-employed consultants; subcontracted and outsourced workers)

Work life changes as organizations become networked. Direct communication becomes possible, and the barriers between ideas and execution disappear. Power is relocated, and a kind of openness and borderlessness are the rules of the day.

These trends lead to a kind of multidimensional virtual culture, and human competence becomes the currency of work. Because of ICT, we can immediately distribute information to our colleagues, through *network management* and *network competency*. And because of this, the core workforce is decreasing – while human competency is key, fewer humans are necessary to get the work done within a company, even as the peripheral workforce is increasing, as companies rely on temporary or agency employees, part-time staff, self-employed consultants, and otherwise subcontracted and outsourced workers.

Our private lives are not immune to these shifts with networking and ICT. *Home becomes a communication center.*

Private life: home becomes a communication center

- The home as the extended family center (on-line families)
- The home as a care center
- The home as a multimedia center
- The home as a center for democratic dialogue
- The home as a marketplace
- The home as a learning center
- The home as a working place – "working from home" and "homing from work" (the role of social media)

The communication circle: the importance of psychosocial communication

Historically, early computers were entirely self-contained and had no communication capability. By the 1970s, computers were used as an information and communication tool and had an impact on communication between humans directly and indirectly, both from a quantitative and qualitative point of view. The concept of the Communication Circle (Figure 2.2) was originally published in Bradley (1977). This initial communication circle is still valid today. The topic of international collaboration and communication in various forms, primarily in the widespread use of Internet and web technology, has become an important component of *sustainability* in workplaces in the ICT society. The message in the communication circle is, in short, that technology directly affects communication because it is a tool and hence influences the structure, quality, and quantity of communication. But it also has an influence on the communication between humans indirectly because of the changes in the phenomena described briefly in the segments of the circle. ICT affects:

- the work content (competence level)
- organizational structure (networks)
- decision support system (centralized or decentralized)
- power structure leadership (power gets invisible, more informal leadership)
- salary and promotion system (revision)
- physio-ergonomic factors (distance)
- possibilities for learning and developing (new incentives to learn)

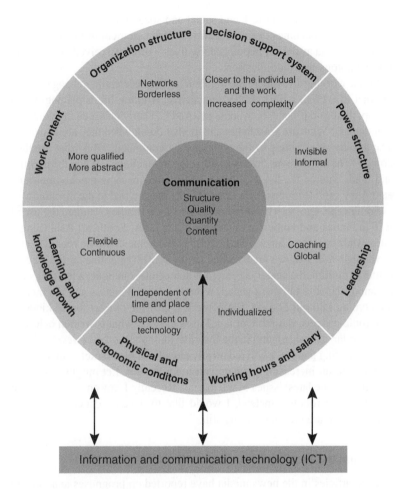

Figure 2.2 The communication circle
Source: (Bradley, 1977, 2006)

These objective factors in the work environment change the communication between people directly and indirectly. The basic thinking reflected in the communication circle turned out to be applicable throughout the continuing technology phases and became fundamental at the introduction and use of the Internet and collaboration in a distributed work environment. In my book (Bradley, 2006) I analyzed the qualitative aspects of communication in large and complex organizations during the third and fourth phases of the evolution of computer technology, including micro computerization and the net era. The widespread use of *social media* during the last few years has dominated the debate on ICT and social and societal change. The communication circle becomes even more current at the moment of the dominance of social media as part of people's daily lives – often perceived as a symbol for technology and digitalization.

In our working lives there are continuous and accelerating changes in the Internet Era. From a little child's perspective, working life is playing with a laptop, iPad, and iPhone, or in some cases a PC. I early on asked my youngest grandchild, "What are your father and mother doing when they are at work?" The answer was "sitting at the computer". I continued, "But what are they doing?" The answer was "writing and going to meetings". When the mobiles and iPads entered the family's home, the answers became quickly multifaceted. Very soon learning involves what functions are tied to the machines.

Some years ago, we (I and my daughter Linda Bradley) studied the use of ICT in homes and home environments in the USA, Southeast Asia (Singapore, Malaysia), and Japan. We found that the home could be regarded as a *communication sphere* – an extended family center (an online family); a care center; a multimedia center; a center for democratic dialogue; a learning center and/or an entertainment center; a marketplace. Business and the market are coming into our homes! The home is a *growing market* for all kinds of electronic gadgets, desirable or not. I used to study what is written below as "Nya Prylar" (new gadgets) in the Swedish journal *Ny teknik* (New Technology). Amazing gadgets – offered mostly already on the market – often disappear due to an increasingly aware consumer market. Let me just list some headlines in the latest issues of the journal. Recently I saw an announcement for "Dancing robots". Instead, I would like to develop dancing skills for humans, who are too often sitting still.

2.3 Humans to robots

Several articles in the news media have reported on prognoses announcing that during the next two decades about 50 percent of the jobs in Sweden will be replaced by digital technology. During the 1970s similar prognoses were presented, but the word "computerization" instead of "digitalization" was used. Many governmental committees were formed to deal with this transformation to work life, employment, vulnerability, security, etc. In the 2020s this whole issue is of a much bigger concern, also involving ethical issues. I will get back to this in the two final chapters of this book.

Brain cells implantation in the robots + Big Data? Use of robots in health care and military? These issues have to be discussed broadly, and both responsible science and responsible citizens are needed. Today, "robotization" is happening in more and more fields, from making cars (such as Nissan's automated factories in Japan) to the military and war (think: drones and rescue robots). The basis was laid early on for a global labor market. At present there is a new discussion on a re-industrialization – due to an increase of salaries in the countries where the corresponding jobs were out-sourced for a couple of years. The robotization taking place worldwide in industry is also contributing to this trend. Creating robots that are human-like is a hot area in computer science and medicine. The ethical problems are huge when it comes to the human-like robots and their planned use in healthcare, elder care and childcare, replacing nurses for certain tasks.

I met the Geminoid-DK robot in Denmark at the Ethics in Computing (ETHICOMP) conference in 2013 (Figure 2.3). This robot was a direct copy of the speaker, associate professor Henrik Scharfe of Aalborg University in Denmark. It was hard to know who would give the talk when you saw them together. And while we may seem to be still walking through the "uncanny valley", where humanoid robots still set off alarm bells, we have come closer to the idea of replacing humans with humanoids. I think we need to reflect more deeply on the use of robots – especially related to the increasing unem-ployment rates around the world – a difficult equation to solve.

The philosopher Michael Lynch, known as a philosopher of truth, has written a book entitled *The Internet of Us: Knowing More and Understand-ing Less in the Age of Big Data*. He starts with a thought experiment describ-ing a society where mini smart phones are hooked directly into a person's

Figure 2.3 Robot at ETHICOMP (2013) Denmark

Photo: Gunilla Bradley

brain as an implant. He argues that when people have for generations lived with these implants, they grow to rely on them to know what they know, and forget how they used to learn for example by observation, inquiry, and reason. Then an environment disaster destroys the electronic communication grid so that the implant crashes. Lynch claims that it would result in a total blindness. No one would really know anything anymore – "no one would know how to know". This is something to ponder at – even if it may look like an extreme story about the future.

2.4 Stress

In next chapter I will outline with graphical illustrations how the ICT society can be viewed and understood, how factors are interacting with the organizations we built over the years and with people, both in a local and global perspective. I will mention some of the human aspects that are sensitive to ICT, among them what we call *stress*.

With ICT our tempo is increasing

New opportunities to work and learn independently of location have changed our *perception of space*. What is expected from us and what we demand from ourselves is increasing all the time – the "level of aspiration" is increasing. People adapt to the machine and its tempo and become unconsciously affected by the *speed* of the machine with indirect effect on the *perception of time*. The words *slowly* and *quickly* have acquired new meanings. The same is true for the words *near* and *far away*. The only thing we cannot buy is time. ICT applications promote short-term rewards and feedback, which seems to be attractive to human nature. Where did longing and yearning go?

"Overstimulation" and "understimulation" are both promoting stress. These two opposites could be balanced by use of ICT. Stress can be characterized by *too much or too little* of various aspects. *Balance of these aspects is desirable. I would call this a society of moderation!* We have to take a position about the following components internet stress.

There are reasons to talk about an Internet stress, due to information overload and contact overload. We are online all the time, which translates into requirements on our availability. No organizational "filters" means it is hard to separate essentials from noise. These newly formed habits lead to the perception that we as individuals have less time and are closer together in physical space. These ICT habits also lead to increased levels of expectations on ourselves and others. 'Multitasking' is a relatively new expression! What will be next?

We have an increased *dependency* on computers and networks, and an increased expectation that these technologies will function well. There is a boom in Sweden and elsewhere on books and courses in "mindfulness" as a tool to handle stress. Maybe people's experiences might be quite different in other countries that have other religious and cultural backgrounds, but I suspect not. International comparative research would be positive in this field. How is stress handled in various cultures, to be preventive as well as in the "here and now"? People are seeking solace in meditation, but is it because they are "on" all the time and never "disconnect" from the Internet and the world? They never have time to "just be me", it seems.

From generation "we" to generation "me"? And back to generation "we"?

My colleagues and I have explored how teenagers in the Nordic countries lived at the turn of the millennium. In 2000, teens were turning from "we" and Nordic cultures of communalism to "me" and the culture of the individual or "individualism". However, "me" could mean many "mes": These teenagers were experimenting with multiple identities, using various avatars to represent them online. Even so, we could see that technology was "keeping the herd together", to use a metaphor. The main changes in human roles at that time period can theoretically be explained, e.g., by "The Convergence Model and Role Formation", which I describe more in detail in Chapter 3. Work environment, home environment, and public environment are converging into a *life environment*, where the public issues tend to merge the private sphere of our homes. Professional role (work life), private role (private life), and citizen's role (public life) converge, forming a *life role*. Effects on the individual become more multifaceted and complex. The *virtual reality* and our participation in cyberspace on various levels are emphasized by embedded technology which makes technology more hidden to the individual and society as a whole. Virtual human roles are being formed and new life styles are created. The following, in short, are the way Lindgren et al. (2005) characterized the MeWe Generation: MeWes are interpersonal individualists; their main goal is to maximize opportunities; friends are what matter: they trust the people they know; they need to stay in constant contact with friends; work is fun and is regarded as an opportunity that opens doors; consumption is an instrument for self-realization and identity experiments and is used for transforming themselves into different personalities.

More recently, teens have been using the Internet to come together into communities again. They want to share all the time. But they are also the "App Generation", meaning that they manage their own lives with apps. They also express the desire and wish that they want the future to be happening now.

As for *teenagers in the USA*, there is kind of new trend. Gautam Malkani, a journalist at the *Financial Times*, has analyzed some recent books to identify trends. One primary issue Malkani identified is that the perennial

power struggle between adolescents and their parents has moved online –
and become a commercial product. Teens can now buy special hardware
and software to escape from parents' control. Instead of trying to evade
online surveillance from governments and corporations, teenagers are more
concerned with avoiding their parents.

I often visit Oman and the Middle East each year to shorten the Nordic winter. I observe another version of being online for teenagers and
especially young women – how a totally closed culture is moving into
the mobile world. I visited Dhofar University in February 2015 and could
imagine the enormous changes that might happen if the authorities do not
tighten/control access to the Internet. But I also noted the trials, and maybe
difficulties, to find one's own way into "the new paradise" while trying to
keep the best part of one's own culture.

2.5 Communication between people

There are many challenges for communication between human beings in
the ICT society (Figure 2.4–2.6). One is *"listening"*, which is the basis for
all other communication. "Meaning" is continuously created by listening.
Listening is the most important communicative quality and ability, and it is
often ignored. Listening means receiving and constructing meaning from
verbal and non-verbal messages. We can think (listen) normally four times
faster than we talk. Listening creates trust, and when trust exists, more
information sharing and more variety occur. By sharing information we win
more insights and hopefully wisdom. Another challenge is *"values"*. They
play a key role for communication – ICT is values-in-action.

Psychologists who study *empathy* are finding that it takes time for the
brain to comprehend the psychological and moral dimensions of a situation.
The more distracted we become and the more emphasis we place on SPEED
at the expense of depth, the less likely we are to *care.*

Dr Yohko Orito of Uppsala University and Prof Kiyoshi Murata of Meiji
University, Tokyo, are warming of the advent of a new type of symptom,
similar to *schizophrenia*, and he refers to research in psychiatry. Unconsid-
ered social media use contributes to *dysfunction of the mental process of the
generation of the Self.* A feeling of strangeness appears that the process of
identity formation has been *taken over by others.* I ask myself if we all are
suffering from a kind of schizophrenia – being in real life (RL) and virtual
reality (VR). Murata points out preventive actions like proper educational
programs, the rights to transparency, and co-ownership of digital objects.
There are *huge changes* due to the use of ICT. There are many *adverse
effects* and also *paradoxes* (Figure 2.4).

This summer I was at an outdoor museum on a beautiful day – but the
others there with me were somewhere else (Figure 2.5)! Do we enjoy these
spaces in the same way (Figure 2.6)?

Figure 2.4 On paternal leave: do we talk with the kids today?
Photo: Gunilla Bradley

Figure 2.5 Visit at a sculpture museum
Photo: Gunilla Bradley

Figure 2.6 Out on an intimate date
Photo: Gunilla Bradley

There are an increasing number of conferences, new journals, reports, and projects, etc., that deal with social impact of new technology. This is especially the case when Internet and web technology were integrated with computer and information technology to form what we call ICT. Media and communication technology became an academic discipline where more and more analyses of the ICT society are based. Often the focus has been on the role of the social media and various applications of social media in society.

At each of my key note presentations in conferences I have thought it was important to cover a broader field and move from the presentations of empirical finds to address some key questions:

How to I perceive the world? – presenting the Convergence Model (Chapter 3)
What is the Good ICT Society? (Chapter 6)
What actions can we take? (Chapter 7)

2.6 Children

Dear Reader, take a look at this cartoon! (Figure 2.7)

Figure 2.7 Children in the old days and now

Source: This work is licensed under a Creative Commons Attribution-Noncommercial 3.0 United States License.

2.7 Summing up

This chapter has hopefully provided you with a view about daily life in most western countries. As I said initially, it is built on a key note presentation that was given at a Vienna Summit 2015. That speech was also filmed by a Swedish film team lead by Karin Wegsjö. The film is available on my homepage (http://gunillabradley.se) under "Short about Gunilla", with some live events in Vienna.

Enjoy!

Note

In 2008 I accepted an invitation to create an international conference within the IADIS umbrella (International Association for Developing the Information Society). I gave it the name of ICT Society and Human Beings, with the purpose of encouraging researchers to explore both the broader changes in the society and the changes for people and the individual. It now serves as a think tank for exploring the psychosocial changes in the society, related to ICT. In 2010 over a period of a couple of years, I invited Diane Whitehouse, present chair of TC9 in IFIP, to co-chair these conferences. By now they become kind of generic type of conference, and the leaders of IADIS http://ict-conf.org have maintained the initial design. An increasing number of participants are contributing to the growth of knowledge in the field. The following are the key words in the conference "call for papers", with the broader themes as a set of headlines, that are all related to the theoretical model that will be presented in Chapter 3.

Bibliography

boyd, d. (2015). *It's Complicated: The Social Lives of Networked Teens*. New Haven, CT: Yale University Press.

Bradley, G. (1977). *Datateknik, arbetsliv och kommunikation. (Computer Technology, Work Life, and Communication)*. The Swedish delegation for long term research. FRN. Liber (in Swedish), Stockholm, SE.

Bradley, G. (1989). *Computers and the Psychosocial Work Environment*. London: Taylor & Francis.

Bradley, G.(2006). *Social and Community Informatics – Humans on the Net*. London/ New York: Routledge.

Bradley, G. (2010). Special Invited Chapter on The Convergence Theory on ICT, Society and Human Beings – towards the Good ICT Society. In: Haftor, D. and Mirijamdotter, A. (eds.), *Information and Communication Technologies, Society and Human Beings – Festschrift in Honor of Gunilla Bradley*. New York: IGI Global, 30–46. ISBN: 978-1-60960-057-0.

Bradley, G. (2014). Social Informatics and Ethics: Towards the Good Information and Communication Society. In: Fuchs, C. and Sandoval, M. (eds.), *Critique, Social Media and the Information Society*. London/New York: Routledge, 91–105.

Bradley, G. (2016). In Search of Wisdom in the ICT Society – Theory and Visions. In: "The Future Information Society: Social and Technological Problems" (Burgin, M. and Bradley, L. (2005). *Home of the Future Japan: Information and Communication Technology (ICT) and Changes in Society and Human Patterns of Behaviour in the Network Era*. KTH Research report ISBN 91-7178-052-1, Royal Institute of Technology (KTH), Stockholm.

Bradley, L. and Bradley, G. (2000). Home of the Future and ICT – Integration of Professional and Private Roles. Special Issue of "Ergonomics", Vol. 43, No. 6 and Included in the Congress CD-ROM Proceedings at the IEA/HFES 2000 Congress, San Diego, USA, Taylor & Francis, London.

Bradley, L. and Bradley, G. (2001). The Home as a Virtual and Physical Space – Experiences from USA and South-East Asia. In: Smith, M.J. and Salvendy, G. (eds.), *Systems, Social and Internationalization Design Aspects of Human – Computer Interaction*. Mahwah, NJ: Lawrence Erlbaum Ass. Inc., 81–85.

ETHICOMP. (2013). The Possibilities of Ethical ICT. University of Southern Denmark, Kolding, Denmark, 12 June–14 June 2013.

Gardner, H. and Davis, K. (2014). *The App Generation: How Today's Youth Navigate Identity, Intimacy, and Imagination in a Digital World*. New Haven, CT: Yale University Press.

Lepore, J. (2016). Review of the Book by Michael Lynch. *The New Yorker*, March 21 2016.

Lindgren, M., Furth, T. and Luhti, B. (2005). *The MeWe Generation*. Stockholm: Bookhouse Publishing.

Lynch, M.P. (2016). *The Internet of Us: Knowing More and Understanding Less in the Age of Big Data*. New York: W.W. Norton.

Orito, Y. and Murata, K. (2014). Dividualisation: Objectified and Partialised Human Beings. Conference paper, CEPE 2014.

Appendix (Chapter 2)

Topics for the ICT society and human beings conference include, but are not limited to

Globalization and ICT

- Globalization processes
- Glocalization processes
- Values, norms
- Labor market (outsourcing, integration, mobility)
- Universal access
- Virtual worlds
- Global villages
- Rethinking economic and social theories
- Human capital theory
- Sustainability, Democracy
- Global catastrophes
- Vulnerability
- Peace and war

Life environment and ICT

- Psychosocial environment
- Work environment/work place
- Quality of working life
- Work content – Work tasks
- Organizational structure
- Decision support systems
- Human-human communication
- Power structure-formal and informal
- Leadership
- Career patterns
- Influence/participation

- Working hours and salary/compensation
- Work pace/work load
- Physical and ergonomic conditions
- Changes in the concept of time
- Changes in the way we are ('being')
- Learning and knowledge growth
- Home environment
- Public environment
- Private environment
- Virtual environment
- Virtual (on-line) communities
- Organizational design and management

Life role and ICT

- Citizen's role
- Professional role
- Leadership role
- Private role
- Virtual roles
- Home of the future
- Mobile life
- Role conflicts

ICT and effects on humans

- Analyses of impact as well as technology contributing to desirable human qualities
- Psychosocial impact
- Life styles
- Human needs (meaningfulness, belonging, autonomy, influence)
- Happiness and fun
- Well-being and health
- Dependency
- Identity
- Integrity
- Trust – security – privacy
- Addictiveness (games)
- Availability
- Motivation
- Human memory

- Cyber sickness
- Stress (over- and understimulation)
- Workload
- Fatigue
- Love and relationships
- Skills and competencies
- Creativity
- Problem solving
- Social competence

Perspectives on ICT

- Social and psychosocial
- Cross-cultural
- Theoretical
- Gender
- Class
- Rural – urban
- Multimodal
- Economic
- Ethical

Desirable goals and ICT

- Integration
- Humanization
- Reducing poverty
- Bridging the digital gap
- Freedom of expression
- Democratization
- E-cooperation
- E-democracy
- Peace
- Sustainability
- Accountability, responsibility
- Involvement, empowerment
- Well-being Health
- Human welfare
- Quality of life
- Human rights

Actions for reaching the Good Information Society

- Individual level
- Community (physical and virtual) level
- Governmental level
- International level
- Civil society and social change in communities
- Design of societal systems – rethinking

3   The convergence model
A path to the golden rule

- What is convergence?
- The main parts of the convergence model
- Effects on human beings
- Dynamics of the model
- Societal self-production
- What is the Good ICT Society?
- From theory and visions to actions
- Bibliography

The summarizing concept for how I perceive the world is convergence or convergence processes. Over the years, starting with my research in the 1970s, I have built the so called convergence model that *synthesizes the framework* in my research on social and psychological life environment and computerization (IT, ICT and digitalization). This model has its roots four decades ago and in research during various phases of the history of computerization. The illustration of the model that I will present in this chapter focuses on *speed and the accelerated process.*

3.1 What is convergence?

Convergence in my model means a movement towards common content. As you can see in Figure 3.1 it becomes another colour, *another shade* at the convergence of the three-dimensional parts. The other parallel process is *interaction*, but the *process of interaction* differs *between authoritarian and democratic societies.*

Convergence occurs in the Network Society where there are *new communication patterns*, for example, direct communication between people, leading to the immediate distribution and exchange of information, and borderless and global communication.

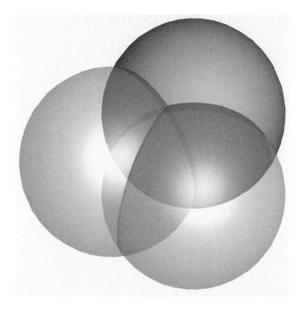

Figure 3.1 Convergence

In networked organizations, power is relocated, a multidimensional virtual culture is developing, and human competence has become the currency, as I discussed in Chapter 2.

3.2 The main parts of the convergence model

Imagine four clusters of overlapping circles, like a three-dimensional Venn diagram. These four clusters of the model are Globalization, Life Environment, Life Role, and ICT (Figure 3.2). The four clusters all interact with each other and at their center are the effects that all four clusters have on human beings. When I illustrate that nexus – the effect on humans – I tend to tell my audience to think of it as a sunflower or exploding star. Those two mental images have very different meanings, which I will come back to later in this chapter. In the meantime, let's break down the four clusters.

Globalization includes three interacting circles: technology, the labour market, and the values and norms that govern these ideas in a society. Globalization also is governed by virtual worlds: we humans interact in online spheres that include the virtual technical infrastructure, virtual labour market, and values connected to these spheres.

The second cluster is the life environment: where work environment (physical as well as psychosocial), home environment, and public

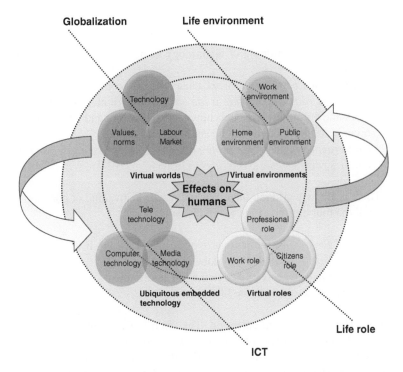

Figure 3.2 Convergence Model on ICT and psychosocial life environment
Source: (Bradley, 2001, 2006, 2014, 2017)

environment interact with each other. Virtual environments interact with these life environments, too, from online games to online team work.

The third cluster is the life role, where convergence between the professional, private and citizenship roles overlap. Of course, virtual roles are played out here too – on social media, professional on-line networks, various platforms and web sites.

The fourth and final cluster is ICT itself, which I illustrate as a convergence of technologies: computer technology, telecommunication technology, and media technology. Here, ubiquitous embedded technology governs and interacts with these circles and the ICT cluster as a whole, including the mobile phones in our pockets and smart chips in passports.

1   *Globalization is convergence* between technology, norms/values (economy), and the labour market.

There are some anti-movements. Values related to the economic system are strong driving forces. Values related to culture and religion operate independently, supportively or oppositional.

2   *ICT (information and communication technology) is convergence* between computer technology, telecommunication technology, and media technology. *(ICT cluster).*
    Ongoing commoning of technology as open source, file sharing, co-production.
3   *Convergence between the work environment, home environment and public environment becomes a life environment* (a cluster), where the work and public environments move into our homes and our homes are brought to the work and public environments.
4   *Convergence between the professional role, the private role, and the citizen's role becomes a life role* (a cluster).

There is a new world out there! *Virtual reality* is invading or converging with all the four clusters. Hence we talk about

1   *Virtual Technology* (ubiquitous, clouds etc.) related to ICT
2   *Virtual Worlds* related to the globalization
3   *Virtual Environments* related to the life environment
4   *Virtual Roles* related to the life role

Virtual Human Roles are emerging. The main tools are the *Internet and web technologies, mobile phones, and new software applications known as social media* (Facebook, Twitter, etc.) that are transforming work, private, and citizen roles. People spend more and more time on the Internet. *In a more extreme form, virtual realities are expressed by another person/ personality* that people take on – for example, *avatars in various online games.* Virtual reality is also reshaping the power *balance between authority and the grassroots and strengthening civil society.*
    We just jump out of and into boxes *in all our roles*; *sometimes half* of us are present. *Presence* in real life has become a luxury, the best gift to "the other" – whether to family, friends, or colleagues!
    Central to all of these interacting spheres (clusters) in this model are the "Effects on Humans" – a sunflower or a circle with double directed arrows in the image shown in Figure 3.2. *The individual* is affected by ICT, life environment, life role, and globalization, but he or she can also influence these areas included the new virtual reality and their convergence with the virtual reality. Effects on the *individual* become *complex.* The way humans *handle* their situations can be either *active or passive.* Examples of active reactions are *involvement, creative behaviour, and protest.* Examples of passive reactions are *alienation, withdrawal,* and *certain psycho-physiological symptoms.*

3.3 Effects on human beings

- Identity and self-perception (*web community identity*)
- Social competence
- Integrity
- Trust (security, privacy – the terms vary)
- Dependency (addictiveness)
- Empowerment
- Empathy
- Stress

There are some aspects that are sensitive to the use of ICT and they are listed above. This conclusion is derived from my own empirical research during four historical periods of computerization, but is also derived from literature reviews conducted during that same time and also conference reports. As a result, these aspects have been taken care of in several policy documents and action plans – both on a national and international level.

How sensitive these human aspects are will be illustrated in my in-depth interviews with people in Chapter 5, "Voices from around the world on quality of life and well-being in the ICT society".

3.4 Dynamics of the model

Each of these clusters interacts with each other, just as the spheres within the clusters feed into each other and change directions. However, the main movement between the clusters (domains) is increasingly affected by changes in society driven by globalization. The movements speed up even more with the accelerating rates of change in research and development in ICT. The interactions between ICT and globalization give a powerful push to the speed of the turning wheels of the whole model. Faster economic transactions, owing to robotization, put the world economy at high risk of collapsing.

Transferring the reasoning to *actions*, we can in our professional role, private role, and/or citizen's role influence our life environment on various levels of analyses, but *an awareness of the speed of change, its causes, and the complexity of our environments* is required.

3.5 Societal self-production

To "*make the complexity simpler*" I would like to refer to the phenomena of "Societal Self-Production" (Figure 3.3). "Human Beings" contribute to

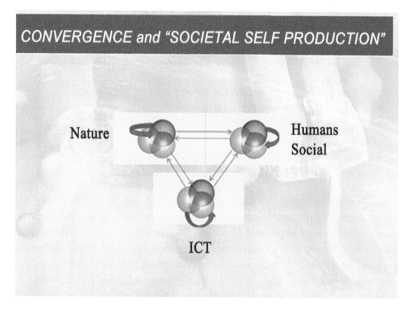

Figure 3.3 Societal self-production
Source: (Bradley, 2014)

the production and reproduction of themselves, including the emergence of the "Social" but also the "Nature" and the artifact "ICT" is more and more reproducing itself. *Everything seems to be interacting with everything.* (From the issue of climate change we can learn much about the digitalization of our lives. We can talk about a kind of "global warming" in terms of the ongoing convergences between the IT, nano technology, biotechnology, artificial intelligence, etc. We get new words and concepts from the field which makes it hard for citizens to take part in the debate and a kind of helplessness develops. However we have "power in the pocket" which we use in the small world, but it has the potential to help us impact on the bigger processes in the society. *In this ambivalent position towards the dialectic reproduction of "physical" and "cultural spheres"* we need an *ethical compass.* This takes us to reflect on what a Good ICT Society is.

3.6 What is the Good ICT Society?

My visions of the Good ICT Society concern the *sunflower* in the middle of the model – the "Effects on Human Beings".

> *Information access for all*
>
> Well-being and *quality of life* for all
>
> Deepening and broadening of *democracy*
>
> *Integration* and respect for *diversity*
>
> *Enrichment* in the social contact between people
>
> Greater *autonomy* for the individual
>
> Prevention of various kinds of overload and stress
>
> E-cooperation and *peace*
>
> Sustainability

Internationally, researchers in ICT formulated *the first official statements* of goals for a Good ICT society at the first World Information Technology Forum (WITFOR) in Lithuania in 2003. The so-called Vilnius Declaration brought forward such goals as *bridging* the digital divide between rich and poor in the world; urban and rural societies; men and women; different generations. Another main concern was *reducing poverty* through the use of ICT. Ensuring the *freedom of expression* was a hot topic and still is. This was the first time that researchers met, and had a dialogue, with politicians on the ministry level from both developed and developing countries. A seed was planted at that time with insights that ICT could be used to broaden and deepen democracy.

WITFOR was followed up by World Summit of the Information Society (WSIS), mainly held in the developing countries where non-governmental organizations and civic society were involved. In the decade following, an *awareness developed around the world* of the *potential connected to ICT.* Examples are the Arabic Spring, Occupy Wall Street, and more.

Thoughts about a good society are not new – there are many examples in politics, religion, and cultural spheres (Figure 3.4 and 3.5).

3.7 From theory and visions to actions

In my presentations over the years I used to play music like "Romance" by the Swedish composer Lars Erik Larsson. Sometimes I played ABBA – "Thank you for the Music" or "Dancing Queen" – for a moment of reflection. And I would present the image of a field of flowers: Future applications are like thrilling seeds. They pop up all the time – *we call them apps* more and more. Some seeds will grow to beautiful flowers – the ones that contribute to fulfill human needs. Then we will have a field of flowers. Basic psychosocial needs can be seen in the flower (Figure 3.6), but the basic physical needs are, of course, fundamental, like food and shelter.

Figure 3.4 The Good Society
Source: (Lorenzetti Sienna 1340)

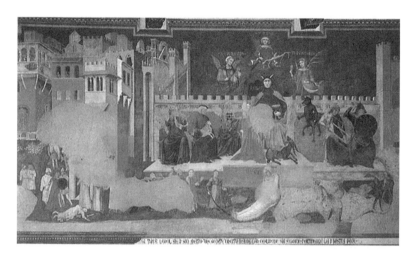

Figure 3.5 The Bad Society
Source: (Lorenzetti Sienna 1340)

The first time I presented this vision of the future, in 2000, and for some years after that, I thought that market forces would regulate the journey, that consumer power would be so strong that we could have a wonderful future with this marvelous technology, increased self-determination and influence, reduced poverty, freedom of speech, and more. At the time, I was at the Telecommunication Department at KTH; *interactivity* was a leading word; the Internet Centre was next door. The School of ICT was formed and next the Centre for Wireless Computing. My close professor colleagues were actually Mr. Internet, Mr. Nanotechnology, and Professor Chip.

Figure 3.6 Human psychosocial needs flower
Source: (Bradley, 2001, 2006)

But today, I wonder whether the beautiful future flowers have withered. The Net has been occupied by terror organizations such as Daesh; there are various instances of misuse and several adverse effects. There is bullying, *hate, sexual abuse, cheating*, and *mutual distrust* due to competing sources of information, etc. *Anonymity and speed* are drivers. In addition there are *cyber-attacks* . . . and risks for a *global cyber war . . . the end of humankind.* Whole societies and civilizations are so *vulnerable* that their *infrastructures* can suddenly be wiped out. I will get back to this in Chapter 4 on ICT in peace and war.

ICT has grown *out of control* for human beings – advanced applications require *wisdom.* There is so much talk about technology development, but nothing about *humane development. Humane development* must be in parallel with technology development. It involves not only intelligence (IQ) but also emotional intelligence and social competence – applied wisdom.

ICT is about "*power*" on various levels or "*politics*" if you want. In theory we are all "empowered". Each one of us can have an impact. Technology has taken a *leap into our hands and pockets.* Have we become more powerful or not? There is an increasing risk of enforcing *centralization, surveillance, and various misuse of power.* The visions and goals for the Good ICT Society for humans need *stronger recognition and actions on all levels of society – including the global level.*

I sometimes feel I have returned to square one, exactly where I started 40 years ago. At that time, a tree of action was needed and applied – the so-called Swedish model was in effect intended to prevent misuse of electronic data processing (EDB) and to guarantee user participation in the design and development of software systems. Time changes everything: A tree of action is needed again with a very strong branch of the tree on the international level, but we also need a strong branch and sub-branches on the *individual level* (see Chapter 7 on actions).

The International Value Map (Figure 3.7), developed by the political scientists Ronald Inglehart and Christian Welzel, helps us to understand cultural complexity and diversity. Traditional versus secular-rational values are mapped against survival versus self-expression values. The map of the world is based on the World Values Survey, which is a global research project that explores people's values and beliefs and how they change over time. Conclusions are also drawn about what social and political impact that the values have. A worldwide network of social scientists have since 1981 conducted representative national surveys in about 100 countries. The map illustrates how closely linked cultural values vary between societies in two main dimensions: Survival values versus self-expression values (x-axis) and traditional values versus secular-rational values (y-axis).

Clusters of countries in the map mirror shared values and not geographical closeness. *Traditional values* emphasize the importance of religion, parent-child ties, respect of authority, principles, and traditional family values. *Secular-rational values* have the opposite preferences to the traditional values. Societies that hold these values place less emphasis on religion, traditional family values, and authority.

Survival values emphasize economic and physical security. They are linked with a relatively ethnocentric view and low levels of trust and tolerance. *Self-expression values* give high priority to subjective well-being, self-expression, and quality of life. Changing from survival values to self-expression values also characterizes the transition from industrial society to post-industrial society, including an emphasis on democratic values.

With globalization, it is increasingly important to understand diversity. People with diverse values will live and work together. Hence it is crucial to understand each others' distinctive worldviews. Self-expression values are considered to be a part of a core value dimension in the modernization process. Self-expression is a cluster of values that include social open-mindedness, life satisfaction, and public expression.

ICT can and should be used to *narrow the gap* between subcultures; it could s*how similarities*, emphasize the *synergy* in the various cultural blocks, and bring us all into a thrilling, fruitful dialogue. We need quite a different *approach. The goal must be "unity and diversity"*. In practice it is important to discuss and develop perspectives on the role of citizens. What competences do we need, how should responsible citizens act in the ICT society, what lifestyles are important? We are all moving toward becoming global citizens.

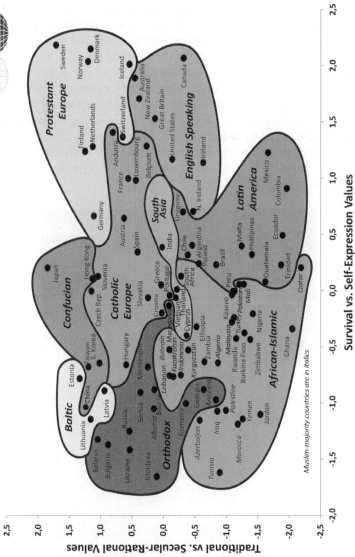

WVS6, 2015

Figure 3.7 The International Value Map

Source: (Inglehart and Welzel, 2015)

"*The Golden Rule*" could serve as a simplified guiding principle. *Maybe we need an app with the Golden Rule. The old creed says, "Treat other people as you would want them to treat you"*. It is sometimes called the law of reciprocity. "The *Distribution issue*" – or the distribution of power and resources – is still a key question and could easily be solved through ICT. *Distribution of resources* is valid for both the *human and the material side. Accumulation of capital and other resources* is speeded up by ICT.

Distribution of resources could also be facilitated by ICT. Think of the possibilities of digital currency such as *Bitcoin*. Every one of us can reflect on what actions we would prioritize in our country, community, work place, and home environment. What do we want to convey to *national and international bodies to act upon?* For many years I kept saying and writing that "*ICT should be used for Deepening our Humane and Societal Qualities*". There is *an inherent opportunity* for the Good and Sustainable Society. What is it all about? I think it is about our *responsibility for the next generation and the planet* (Figure 3.8).

Figure 3.8 Sustainability
Photo: Gunilla Bradley

Note

For a quick presentation of my theory I have made the chapter short, but would like to refer to two appendixes. In Appendix 1 I refer to an analysis of relation to some of Marx´s concepts and in Appendix 2 I refer to an analysis of relation to classical theories on the information society.

Bibliography

Bradley, G. (1989). *Computers and the Psychosocial Work Environment*. London: Taylor & Francis.

Bradley, G. (ed.). (2001). *Humans on the Net: Information and Communication Technology (ICT) Work Organization and Human Beings*. Stockholm, SE: Prevent. ISBN 91-7522-701-0.

Bradley, G. (2006). *Social and Community Informatics-Humans on the Net*. London/New York: Routledge.

Bradley, G. (2011). The Convergence Theory on ICT, Society and Human Beings: Towards the Good ICT Society. In: Haftor, D. and Mirijamdotter, A. (eds.), *Information and Communication Technologies, Society and Human Beings*. New York: IGI Global, 30–46.

Bradley, G. (2014). Social Informatics and Ethics: Towards the Good Information and Communication Society. In: Fuchs, C. and Sandoval, M. (eds.), *Critique, Social Media and the Information Society*. London/New York: Routledge, 91–105.

Bradley, G. (2015). TED-Talk on YouTube Understanding the Change of Habits in the ICT Society. http://tedxtalks.ted.com/video/Understanding-the-Change-of-Hab

Bradley, G. (2016). In Search of Wisdom in the ICT Society – Theory and Visions. In: Burgin, M. and Hofkirchner, W. (eds.), *The Future Information Society: Social and Technological Problems*. World Scientific, 123–136.

Danielsson, U. (2007). *Relationships between Information Communication Technology and Psychosocial Life Environment: Students and Young Urban Knowledge Workers in the ICT-Era*. Doctoral dissertation at Department of Informatics, Mid Sweden University.

Inglehart and Welzel (2015). The International Value Map. Recreation of the 2010 map. https://en.wikipedia.org/wiki/Inglehart%E2%80%93Welzel_cultural_map_of_the_world https://en.wikipedia.org/wiki/Human_Development_Index

Swingle, M. (2006). *I-Minds: How Cell Phones, Computers, Gaming, and Social Media are Changing Our Brains, Our Behavior, and the Evolution of Our Species*. British Columbia: New Society Publishers.

Appendix 1 (Chapter 3)

I would like to add a section from my chapter in a book by Christer Fuchs and Marisol Sandoval (Editors), **Critique, Social Media and the Information Society** *(London/New York: Routledge, 2014). I relate the convergence model to Marx's concepts that had been discussed at an international conference at Uppsala University, May 2012.*

There are several Marxist concepts that can be related to the convergence model:

1 *Globalization cluster*: ICT speeds up capital accumulation, which is met by new forms of global actions and revolts. It is possible to observe a new form of the exploitation of labor, due to an ICT related blurring of work life and private life as well as a marginalization of labor through exclusion. The so called *playbour* needs a thorough analysis coupled to the economic system.

2 In the *ICT cluster*, there is an ongoing *commoning* of technology, for example in the case of open source, file sharing, and other new forms of co-producing and sharing of knowledge, which are driving forces in laying a base for the reconstruction of the life environment and possible seeds of a non-proprietary and more collaborative form of economy (Benkler, 2006).

3 *Life environment cluster* (life sphere): at the convergence of four components (work environment, private environment, public environment, and virtual environment), diversified struggles are going on. *Prosumption* seems to be a new environment/sphere – it is neither work nor private or public, which results in a corresponding new life role of the prosumer.

4 *Life role cluster*: Humans are trying to find a *balance* between the converging human roles in spite of new facilitating technology. Early in our research we could report that a growing part of the labor consists of part-time staff, self-employed consultants, sub-contracted and outsourced workers, and temporary and agency employees. Some of these are key resources, while others are exchangeable but both are very loosely tied

into the welfare system. They are sometimes called *free agents/free lancers/portfolio individuals.* This could be compared with *Precarious workers* and the Precariat (originating from Proletariat), expressions used within postmarxistic literature and in some current news media.

5   *Effects on humans*: The multifaceted effects on humans can be structured in passive reactions and active reactions. *Alienation*, withdrawal, some psychosomatic syndromes are examples of passive reactions. Active reactions have acquired new arenas through the virtual world and the social media. Social protest movements of various kinds are operating both on "the streets" and in VR and in the digital sphere.

The concept of exploitation is complex. Who is exploiting whom? What part of society forms the exploiter? What levels of analysis need to be taken into account? Can we talk about an interactive and mutual exploitation? What role has the growing amount of small entrepreneurs in the labor market?

To be able to analyse the present trends and the future, you need to go back to basics, explore the work content, work organization, salary policy/ principles, working hours, communication patterns, reward systems etc. and develop adequate concepts. The concept of digital labor is too broad and vague. Listening, observing, recording, structuring, refining and developing concepts are crucial processes. Social psychologists, sociologists, political scientists, computer scientists, national and global economists, micro and macro economists have to meet and listen to each other. A broad spectrum of tools is possible for modeling, collecting and analysing information of various kinds – across cultures and political systems. Research is not value free but value rich. The only way to approach this is in dialogue.

Processes like psychosocial, alienation, liberation, globalization, reification, commodification and commoning need to be analysed and described for present conditions. Research on this could also be added to a new Wikipedia entry on "ICT and Marxism".

Parts of my early empirical research were done during a time when Sweden tried to balance two political systems. And the main focus in society was that computers should be a tool to rationalize work and working life. A vision dominated that work and production life should play a smaller part of people's life. I started my research when Sweden served as a kind of model country for balancing capital and labor. In 1968, when the worldwide student revolt took place, I was at the Department of Sociology at Stockholm University. The whole university was a battle field, comparable to other campuses in Europe and USA. The theoretical framework and concepts I developed were close to the vocabulary that workers and employees used in the working places and that also were mirrored in the public debate and in next step in laws and agreements. I can refer in this context to my 2006 book (Routledge 2006).

Within "Swedish socialism" as well as social democracy that was in power back then, the traditional Marxist concepts were considered as being outdated. The former Soviet Union was close to the Swedish border and people were looking at Soviet socialism with disgust and fear. Countries like Cuba, Israel with its kibbutzim, and Yugoslavia with its worker owned companies were in contrast at the time giving some hope for left wing young students. Ironically Sweden was closer than most European countries to a far reaching socialism, with preparations for introduction of economical democracy, so-called "löntagarfonder". However these plans were closed soon after the fall of the Wall and the whole economic system went global and Sweden moved "to the right" partly due to an extreme dependency on export industries.

Over the years I used to argue that "computerization" will utmost result in a huge "allocation problem" (see Chapter 7).

In 2014 I concluded:

- Accumulation of capital and a search for the cheapest and most competent labor is a fast and accelerating process
- The algorithm for the accumulation of capital can also be used for the allocation of capital and competence and further allocation of resources with the same speed and targets.
- The danger is that investments in wisdom and in a humanizing process, attending to the everyday quality of life of people, has not been taken place before this "turn around".

Appendix 2 (Chapter 3)

*I would like to add a section from my chapter in a book by Darek Haftor and Anita Mirijamdotter (Editors), **Information and Communication Technologies, Society and Human Beings – Theory and Framework, Honoring Professor Gunilla Bradley** (IGI Global, 2011). I analyze how the convergence theory of ICT and the psychosocial life environment, relates to other theories about the information society and provided an abbreviated summary of classical theories in the area of the information society and several perspectives of the work life environment.*

Classical theories of the information society

In answer the question posed in the title of this section, I want to refer to Frank Webster's (1995) *Theories of the Information Society* that is an interrogative and skeptical view of the concept of an 'Information Society'. He presents five definitions of the information society that represent criteria for the new society (technology, economy, occupation, space, and culture) and analyses contemporary social theories rather than the social impacts of technology. A 'pro-Information Society perspective' means that the theory offers hypotheses that posit a clear shift to something new, to a quite different type of society. An 'anti-Information Society perspective' are a group of theories that argue that structures and processes have been maintained and that there is no need talk about a new era of 'Information Society'. Frameworks and terminologies associated with pro-Information Society perspectives are post-industrialism, postmodernism, flexible specialization, and the information mode of development. Frameworks and terminologies regarded as anti-Information Society theories include: neo-Marxism, regulation theory, flexible accumulation, the nation-state and violence, and the public sphere. I briefly summarize the main content of these five theories according to Webster.

Giddens (2000) argues that the origins of today's 'information societies' are to be found in surveillance activities driven principally by the requirements of a world organized into nation-states. The modern world consists of nations that are 'information societies' and have always been so, but need even more to maintain allocative resources such as planning and administration, authoritative resources such as power and control, and information which is the core of modern military affairs.

Giddens recognizes that information per se has great importance in society, but contends that the significant character of society is continuity, that patterns and structures in society reappear, and that ICT does not challenge those patterns and structures.

According to Schiller's (1993) Critical Theory, labeled neo-Marxism, ICT is essential for the stability and health of the economic system. He concludes that ICT is controlled by corporate capitalism and international empires, market criteria, and consumerism, which means that it is necessary to sell a global life style. Information is a commodity. Consequently, he asks: For whose benefit and under whose control is ICT implemented? The strength of Schiller's argument lies in his presentation of alternative ways of organizing society and in his contention that the information society has a real human history developed by social forces.

Habermas (1989) fears that the public sphere – the independent arena where public opinion was formed over a period of about 100 years and of major importance to the proper conduct of democraciesis – is being diminished. The quality of information determines the health of the participants. ICT emphasizes commercial principles and systems of mass communication. Information content is characterized by actions, adventure, trivia, and sensations.

The 'Regulation School' addresses theories about how a capitalist system achieves stability. Fordism (Keynesianism of the industrial society) has evolved to post-Fordism which is characterized by globalization of markets, production, finance, and communication; corporate restructuring (e.g., downsizing, outsourcing, ICT infrastructure, less mass production); flexible specialization; and effects on labour (e.g., flexibility of employees, wage flexibility, time flexibility).

Postmodernism posits a new type of society; a paradigm shift has taken place. According to Barthes, reality is primarily a matter of language and discourse; hence, the world is informational. For Baudrillard, culture is one important sign of the Information Society; however, the signs are simulations not representations and there is no distinction between the real and unreal or the true and false. Vatimo believes that the expansion of media creates multi-perspectivism. Lyotard argues that knowledge and information is treated as a commodity; truth is replaced by a plurality of truths; requirements for new skills emerge; and life-long education becomes necessary.

Webster argues that, nonetheless, characteristics of capitalist continuity in the society remain. At the same time, however, there is a shift in orientation to a novel form of work organization and to changes in occupational patterns. He concludes that there has been no system break.

Finally, a summary of theories of the Information Society must mention the possibly most comprehensive contribution in the last decade, Castells's (1996–1998) triology *The Information Age: Economy, Society, and Culture*. These volumes represent a 'life work' that is comparable to Marx's *Das Kapital*. Not only is the trilogy deeply theoretical, it presents empirical data to support all the reasons to dicuss a Net society. Nor can we ignore Jensen's (1999) discussion of the Dream Society which represents the end of humankind's multimillenium epoch of material domination and he predicts the beginning of the first post-materialistic era. He organizes the most important raw materials of the twenty-first century into four eras: agricultural (soil, fields, livestock); industrial (coal, oil, steel); information (data, information, knowledge); and dream (pictures, stories, myths, legends). He emphasizes that the raw materials that dominate in the dream era are also available in less-developed countries like African countries, India, along the Polar Circle, and the Pacific Islands.

My own perspective on this complex issue is an integration of both 'pro-Information Society' and 'anti-Information Society' theories. In the short run, the development of the society may appear as a continuation according to Giddens. But in a market-driven globalized world there will be an antithesis, a stage where a paradigm shift occurs that results in a deeper rethinking in order to ensure the survival of society. The network society in its various shapes alters the basis for individual and societal identities. Web communities are bringing together people across new dimensions. The prerequisites for informal power are growing and power will not be associated with capital to the same degree as it currently is. The costs of empowering people with knowledge capital are gradually being reduced. The economic crisis in 2009 has increased awareness of societal vulnerability (the speed of the recession process was ICT-related).

Another general comment on the relationship between Convergence Theory and the more macro-level theories summarized above is that the introduction and use of ICT in the home environment should not be left to governance steering factors that have been present in work life. A cross-disciplinary research program is called for and should be integrated with full-scale models for various applications. Basic human needs and 'people push' technology not 'technology push' should be guiding principles.

Theories of working life

Theories that more directly relate to the corporate world and working life in a broad sense come from many academic disciplines and academic communities, cultures that have different perspectives and focuses. What are the contributions from the information systems community? For many years the focus was on the *development and design* of information systems and later on the *introduction and use* of information systems. The tele-technology and media technology parts of the ICT concept were not addressed for many years. Some contributions after 2000 are the following:

Melville et al. (2004) developed a model of IT business value and thereby chose a resource-based view of the firm, which is often used in management literature and international business. They applied their integrative model to synthesize research about IT business value and developed propositions for future research in the field. Their conceptual model is comprehensive and shows the complexity of the field. Although integrative, it is, however, not interactive in the sense that interaction between theoretical levels of analysis is discussed. The main concepts are resources in the form of technological IT resources, human IT resources, and complementary organizational resources. The other concepts are business processes and performance with a focus on the competitive environment: industry characteristics, trading partner resources, and business processes. Within a macro environment are country characteristics and similar concepts.

Schulze and Orlikowski (2001) explored the discourse on virtual organizing and identified a number of metaphors that characterize various aspects of virtuality. They examined the various metaphors in the practitioner-directed literature on virtual organizing and concluded that the discourse contained a multiplicity of different metaphors, such as virtual organizing as a platform, existing in space, composed of bits, operating as a community and engaging in a network of relationships. They suggest that, due to the absence of experiences to guide practice, these images shape people's views of and actions towards virtual organizing. They then analyzed these metaphors with regard to type of organizing, meaning, source, examples, affordance, and challenge. Their conclusion that metaphors are powerful tools of social construction suggests that researchers and practitioners must be aware of their critical implications and unintended consequences.

Another strand of research in the information systems literature is user acceptance theory (Davis et al., 1989). Van der Heijden (2004) discusses the differences in user acceptance models for productivity-oriented and pleasure-oriented information systems, hence emphasizing various values.

Values focused research can also be found in the formation of world-wide networks of various ICT-related academic schools that share some common perspective (e.g., Network for Value Sensitive Design; Community Informatics Research; The International Conference on the Social and Ethical Impacts of Information and Communication Technologies; International Association for Developing the Information Society; and the ICTs and Society Network).

Critical research has been more common outside the information systems community but this is changing. According to Walsham (2005), a critical approach is a perspective that includes, for example, the social construction of 'truth', historical and cultural contingency, and power relations. He argues that there is a need for information systems research that is critical and is aimed at creating a 'better world' with technology. He draws implications for action in terms of a research agenda, teaching activities, publishing, and institution building. A 'better' world with ICT should not mean better in purely economic terms but also related globally to social and spiritual welfare. He concludes that global futures in general and the information systems field in particular are not pre-determined but result from our own efforts and actions.

4   Toward peace on earth

It may sound strange to talk about World Peace and ICT, but I think that the two go hand in hand. In my work, I have written a lot about convergence and what I see as everyone's responsibility for the next generation and for the planet. We are all global citizens. And we all are living lives that have both virtual and real aspects (Figure 4.1).

We global citizens have to unite, and we have to unite our virtual and real selves. We need peace – in the real world, in ourselves, in our real lives, and in relation to each other.

I first presented the ideas that follow at the IFIP World Computer Congress in Zurich in 2002. IFIP is a global non-governmental organization for researchers and professionals working in the field of ICT.

At the time, I felt optimistic about the world, but the situation has since changed. More conflicts have developed, including the Syrian local conflict that developed into a war, resulting in a wave of migration comparable to the one that followed the Second World War.

On the 70th anniversary of the end of the Second World War, Swedish radio and television broadcast a lot of programs and documentaries, especially on the similarities between 2015 and the earlier period. Unemployment, disaffected youth, populism, nationalism, "ethnic cleansing" in various locations – these are some of the similarities that exist between the way people think and act today and the way they thought and acted more than 70 years ago.

Figure 4.1 Peace building
Photo: William Petersson

We are still human beings. With the advent of ICT, the conventional wisdom has been that technology will unite us. It will promote freedom of thought in places where despots and fascism have ruled. But we also have to remember that ICT can give rise to cyberwarfare, in all aspects of our lives – not just cyberattacks against banks or hacking, but also the kinds of attacks against infrastructure that threaten our everyday ways of life. I argue here that, in order to have a peaceful life assisted by ICT, we have to think of the possibility of war via ICT, and how to prevent it.

Overall, ICT can help to reduce risks by enhancing discussion between people. The ultimate goal is to build a Good Information and Communication Society. In principle, this should be easy – since all people want to live a peaceful life. Positive actions to build peace and to avoid war have to be taken by each and every one of us. Peace builds inside each of us as individuals. Every human being has to combat the destructiveness of the opposite condition: that war also starts within us. Hence, we have to struggle hard to counterbalance these two trends and yearnings.

I have thought about these issues and the different ways that ICT can be used as a tool of war but also of peace. In the following pages, I've tried to distill these issues. After decades of consideration, I have arrived at a list of four principal domains for positive action: awareness-building, education and development, software and games, and adoption of an international perspective.

We read every day in the newspapers and online media that cyberattacks are occurring in the financial sector and the exact number of people affected by them is unknown. What is happening within banks is kept hidden because it would expose their weaknesses vis-à-vis their competitors and would influences levels of trust. There are similarities in what I have come to think of as ICT "war and peace": cyberattacks are not made evident to the public. It would undermine the level of trust on which society is built. If attempts to attack ICT infrastructure were to be reported to people in the mass media, it would undermine society.

Only recently have some of these attacks come to light, and possibly only out of necessity: for example, on 19 May 2016, Arlanda and Bromma airports in Sweden had to ground all planes because of what turned out to be a lapse due to maintenance by the telecommunications company. It affected the computer systems that allow air traffic controllers to see and direct planes in air space. This happened at the same time that an EgyptAir flight disappeared over the Mediterranean sea. People made discomforting connections between the two events, whether or not they were related in reality. Was it a cyberattack? In the previous weeks, major newspaper sites in Sweden were also hacked and "went dark" for hours. These are obvious attacks. How many more go unseen? How do we prepare for and prevent these battles in the ICT cyberwars?

4.1 Some observations on ICT, war, cyber warfare, and infrastructure

War is scarcely a new phenomenon. In its early stages, it was associated more with aggressive or military raids of one tribe against another. More recently, many of the most destructive wars in human history took place in the 20s century. This growth in destructiveness is assumed to be due directly to the expansion and the efficiency of the technologies used, including, before the First World War, the growth in many instruments and technologies, including tanks and flight (Europe 1900–1914) and, at the end of the Second World War, the use of the atomic bomb. These are reflections and conclusions reached after a reading of texts to be found on Wikipedia, for example, on peace-building, pre-requisites for peace, and war.

Two counterbalancing approaches appear to be necessary. First, it is now imperative to study how war takes place and by what methods. Second, it is vital to investigate and to learn about the means to resolve the human tendency to want to go to war and how to grow beyond war's basis in conflict. Only in this way can nations be restored to conditions under which they respect and honor peace (Höglund & Fjelde, 2011).

War is state-based organized violence, but there are many other examples of potential and actual violence that are coming to the fore today. Many ad hoc groups are involved in the use of violence whether for "need, greed or creed" a phrase first used by William Zartmann, professor at Johns Hopkins

University in 2004. While violent actions may come from individuals, loosely organized groups or organized crime, they can also emerge from autocratic and other types of states. There will always be countries and regimes interested in taking advantage of instability in other nations with the expectation that they can shape stability in their own country.

Critical information infrastructures can be used to both support warfare and avoid war. They could also create that instability, not just take advantage of it. Aspects of security that support this infrastructure can be called "cyber security", and they can help to maintain both national and international security. However, cyber security can also be used for both espionage and sabotage.

Some uses of ICT pose threats of quite new dimensions, whether as a result of conscious intent, error or ultimately through the very vulnerability of ICT (Berleur et al., 1993). It is all too horribly easy to imagine an extreme, and potentially final, catastrophe that could result, for example – whether deliberately or *ad hoc* – from today's combination of weapons such as ICT and nuclear power. Perhaps a hacker could find the launch codes for the nuclear missiles stored across the interior of the USA, or a visiting scientist might steal plans or plant computer viruses in a lab in Iran.

Indeed, while it can be said that nuclear power is only usable and controllable through the use of ICT, ICT's shortcomings can lead to errors, failures, and disasters not only in the nuclear domain but also in many other fields (Kajtazi, 2012). Of course, atomic and other crises may occur as a result of natural and unanticipated phenomena. Environmental disasters can happen as a result of solar flares (for example, interfering with satellite signals), or perhaps, earthquakes or tsunami or even together, as happened in Tokohoku-Oki in 2011 tsunami, when an earthquake triggered a tsunami that then melted down a nuclear power plant. That disaster sent nuclear contamination around the world, lofted by the wind into the atmosphere.

In contemporary society, particularly in developed countries but also increasingly in emerging economies, critical infrastructures based on ICT can be conceived as fundamental to the capacity to live in peace and prosperity. Almost all domains of people's lives are dependent on ICT – a situation that we may wish to avoid or at least to counterbalance. Society is so reliant on the use of ICT and its critical infrastructures that the collapse of these systems could leave whole populations without structures, services, and applications. Sheer demand, resulting from the expected growth in consumption, may have dire consequences for the capacity to continue to provide energy supplies.

Imagine a hack that takes down the metro system in your town, plus all the traffic lights. That development alone would lead to traffic snarls, delayed deliveries of food, medicines, and other necessities. Consider the number of lives that could be lost in hospitals or perhaps in traffic accidents.

Now imagine that it is not just the metro, but also the emergency services, flight control systems, communications between banks and clients, heating and water purification systems, and so on. Everything is reliant on interconnections in one way or another, and if all the technologies go down at once, then what?

This generalized movement towards complete ICT dependency could mean that entire societies and nations could collapse with great speed, if ever there were to be a massive failure in their ICT infrastructures. At best, people's working and personal lives will be disrupted. At worst, that failure could be an attack meant to quickly destroy or render inoperable whole societies and civilizations through their infrastructures.

This kind of crisis could inhibit the ability to communicate among family members, friends, and acquaintances. In several crises during the past few years, people have relied on Facebook communication – for example, during the bombings in Brussels in 2016, the online platform practically forced users to report that they were okay – or tried to phone family members during the aftermath of Hurricane Katrina, when phone services were overwhelmed in 2005.

These events can stem from terrorist attacks as well as natural causes. Either way, they could also impair the continuity of human existence in those communities that are located in either very hot or very cold climates or countries that experience both extreme heat and cold. Therefore the general implications for peace and harmony are considerable, since many of these threats could lead to complete societal breakdown. This challenge is perhaps particularly hard for everyday people and policymakers to envision.

ICT is directly implicated in these risks. Instead, in the ICT era, awareness of societal vulnerability should be a notion that unifies all nations.

Research on sustainability from various perspectives could also be undertaken in many institutions; however, sustainability on the one hand and peace/warfare on the other are often not addressed together. The missing perspective is the relationship between environmentalism and wars. Wars are the worst activity to destroy nature. This also holds true for psychosocial and environmental sustainability, so to speak. But wars are not addressed in the same way as the big issues in the environmental discussion, from climate change to chemical contaminants – and ICT fits into these issues as well, from e-waste to mining impacts. In my mind, war is a total collapse in the ambition to create a sustainable society. In addition, violence creates more violence.

4.2 Researching and reporting on ICT and war

More and more institutions are dealing with combating warfare and building peace, increasingly focusing on international and national aspects of cyber warfare. Research institutions, government organizations and the news media are picking up on these issues – and each of these will have an impact on how we as individuals and a society will respond to these questions.

On a global level, the United Nations works on such tasks (Doyle & Sambrinis, 2006) and each nation has its own similar institutions that research these challenges at some level or in some aspect.

To take the Scandinavian countries as just one example, they now have a variety of peace research institutes: Norway's Peace Research Institute Oslo; Sweden's Stockholm International Peace Research Institute; Folke Bernadotte Academy in Stockholm, which also active in the fields of peace, security, and development; and finally the Uppsala University Department of Peace and Conflict Research (UDPCR), plus its Peace Research Programme.

The first is known for both its basic research and its policy-relevant research and the way in which it has engaged itself in promoting peace through the resolution of conflict by means of dialogue, reconciliation, public information, and policy-making. The second is an internationally renowned think tank. As an independent international institute dedicated to research into conflict, armaments, arms control and disarmament, it bases its work on openly available data sources. The third has a research programme on governance, conflict, and peace-building.

During my final review of this chapter, I made some additional research and found a very interesting and important YouTube clip, a 10 minute-long interview with Professor Peter Wallensteen of the Peace and Conflict Research Department at Uppsala University. That video led me also to the home page of *Uppsala Conflict Data Project (UCDP)* UDPCR where there were links to several events that occurred during 2015–2016, that were possible for anyone to listen to and learn from. Three items caught my special attention.

First, UCDP is a unique resource. Scholars can now follow and study local, sub-national or trans-national conflicts in vast areas of the globe and over a very long time period. UCDP data is built to be globally comparable. The data that are collected for each incident includes: Location as to day and village level, date of event when started and ended, info about who died (civilian, military, rebel, other), and reference to sources. The dataset includes 105,000 events of organized violence and covers Africa, Asia, and the Middle East with the exception of Syria.

Second, Professor Wallensteen has published a new book *Quality Peace: Peace Building, Victory, and World Order* that deals with what happens after war ends and how to reach more quality peace.

Third, researchers at the department have presented *nine recommendations for strengthening the efforts for achieving global peace*, after extensive discussions within the department. Their recommendations were in short that we have to:

- Actively contribute to the UN's peace building work
- Strengthen efforts for international mediation
- Interrupt the conflict spirals through concrete peace creation
- Provide psychological and social support to people traumatized by war
- Work towards improved tolerance and broadmindedness
- Promote democracy and good governance
- Invest in education and learning
- Working for increased equality
- Fight poverty and promote inclusive world economy.

The daily press reports new European and international collaborations initiated with the purpose of defending nation states and preventing new potential catastrophes (see www.svd.se/cyberattackerna-visar-var-sarbarhet or www.svd.se/sverige-bland-de-bast-rustade-for-cyberkrig). But nations also are investing in cyber security, and one might argue that peace depends on this, at least to some extent. However, starting in 2013, revelations from Julian Assange and WikiLeaks (https://wikileaks.org) and later by the American computer programmer Edward Snowden show how extensive surveillance has become of people and organizations. The leaking of continuous information about new "cybercrimes", and the ways in which various national authorities are monitoring them, seems to have contributed to a kind of paranoia among the "good guys" as well as in society as a whole. Increased surveillance creates even more surveillance by more and more people.

   The long-term impact that these two whistle blowers, Assange and Snowden, have had both on politics and on people's mindsets are not yet possible to determine, but most likely the effects vary according to the part of the world and the type of nation state. It depends on whether people trust their governments or not. But the fact that digital footprints exist is a fact. Sessions and panels at many international conferences now deal with the topic of "After Snowden" (e.g., ISIS Summit Vienna 2015, "The Information Society at the Crossroads, Response and Responsibility of the Sciences of Information"), which indicates the academic interest in the subject. The American political thriller *Snowden* from 2016 and the thriller film about Julian Assange, *The Fifth Estate* from 2013, encapsulating the way in which they were looked on at the time, and the impacts they have had, also attest to the public fascination with these two men and their exposés of previous secrets.

   In March 2012, the European Commission launched a proposal for a European Cyber Crime Centre to tackle cybercrime (European Commission,

2012). Cybercrime is essentially seamless or borderless. Its perpetrators do not care about the locations and countries of the victims of their crimes. This European center, located in The Hague in the Netherlands, gathers together some of Europe's brightest minds in cyber security. Its task is to warn the European Union Member States about any major cyber threats that are on the horizon and any weaknesses in their online performances. It works on identifying crime by discerning patterns in attacks by computer viruses, for example.

Groups of Scandinavian (and other) investigators have also explored the growth in profiling by corporations, tracking of suspects, electronic tagging of prisoners at work, and the monitoring of pedophilia, money-laundering, information warfare, and cybercrime. They have also assessed the benefits and costs of surveillance, and its future developments (Ball & Webster, 2003).

In parallel with a focus on cyber-attacks and prevention of cyber war, traditional and extremely cruel warfare is ongoing at the borders of European Union. The civil war in Syria became a war involving many nations. A couple of big global players in the region are indirectly involved. The terrorist organization called ISIS (Daesh) has become another player. Through its rhetoric and its cruel actions, ISIS seemed to make it possible for former enemies to talk with one another for a certain time span. In Ukraine it looks like cyber space is used to conduct an "information war". The fighting groups are receiving quite different versions about reality – one might call it propaganda.

In France, a phenomenon known as "dangerization" is discussed that would lead to a kind of total "infantilization", in which many events and occurrences are portrayed as dangerous so that all people are encouraged to protect, and even over-protect, themselves; children are constantly monitored by their parents and remain in continuous contact with them even also as grown adults. One big question arises: precisely what skills are required in today's society so that we do not end up in a situation of complete helplessness and loss of empathy.

Huge waves of migration, with people on the move aiming to escape not only from the conflict and war in Syria but also poverty and violence in many nations in Africa, show the different impacts that ICT can have: immigrants can tap into navigation apps and maps online, communicate with each other, and find out where is "best" to go – these developments too will impact the rest of the world. Researchers repeatedly try to catch the migration flow with illustrations of size and origin of the mass of people moving. Migration is at a very dramatic stage and people are suffering.

The news media have ambitions to describe the details of the war, as if it were an ongoing drama. I find something "very sick" about this dramatic portrayal, including the handling of weapons, in addition to dismay about the difficulties in reaching an agreement in Europe regarding migration policy. Various broadcasts and other media play a role in the messaging about this domain in terms of the ways in which they present developments in warfare to the public; they are becoming more and more explicit in terms of the images used to depict war, death, violence and injury. Beyond this, the media are influential in the manner in which they encourage children, young people and adults to view – and even potentially get involved in – violence, aggression, and even war. Violent content receives less attention than sexual content or bullying in awareness-raising initiatives. Many children express shock on witnessing violent and aggressive online content, especially graphically depicted and realistic violence against vulnerable victims (Livingstone et al., 2011 and Livingstone, 2014).

Both Sweden and Norway have experienced terrorist threats recently. In continental Europe, Paris and Brussels were cruelly attacked, in 2015 and 2016, by members of the same group of militant Islamists. These events, the way they were portrayed in media, and how ICT intersected to both help and hinder them are all important opportunities for field studies in peace research with focus on terrorism and Internet war with a broader analytical perspective.

Academic disciplines tend to be born in the search for solutions to a specific problem, but then they take on a life of their own. The bodies set up to examine problems related to peace and war might be quite distant from the people and the victims themselves. Swedish television rarely interviews personnel from any of the relevant peace research institutes, with a view on the struggles going on in the world. Very often it is the ministers or politicians who have a voice. Journalists and peace researchers could collaborate. The problems they will face in getting the information they need are the close connections to police, military, and security issues on various levels and areas that tend to secrecy.

War and terrorism are not the only way to gain exposure to violence in the ICT context. A Swedish Media Council report in 2011 examined a decade of work on the part of several international expert bodies (including the USA Department of Health and Human Services and children's medical associations in Australia, Canada and the USA). Collectively, these studies take the stance that very violent games increase the likelihood of aggressive behavior. In an article that followed in the *Dagens Nyheter*, three researchers debated these challenges (Olsson et al., 2012). They agreed that it is not easy to distinguish violent games as the unique factor that generates violence and aggressiveness in young people. Among stronger predictors of violence are the four elements of family relationships, genetic disposition, personality, and socialization. However, for children who have grown up in an environment where interpersonal violence is normal and even prevalent, violent games offer yet another source of learning how to behave aggressively and stifle empathic development.

The notion of "game dependency" has to be considered in-depth through research, study, and discussion on the relationship between violent computer games and aggressive behavior. Similarly, research indicates a gradual loss of empathy alongside extreme use of mobile phones (Konrath et al., 2011; Zaki, 2011). This too deserves in-depth investigation (Zaki and Ochsner, 2012).

4.3 Starting to study the problems

There are certainly plenty of theoretical questions that can be studied in the fields of research on war, peace, and violence. Many of the issues raised and questions posed in these fields, and their institutes, are based on experiences with conflicts that have either occurred or are ongoing.

Based on discussions first initiated in July 2011 in Rome, Italy, at the International Association for the Development of the Information Society (IADIS) ICT, Society and Human Beings conference (Bradley et al., 2011), I and my colleagues proposed a first set of questions that could be posed by experts who work within the field of studies on ICT and warfare. We attempted to formulate a number of questions that can help analyzing issues that are a contemporary threat to peace. The topics listed struck us as already deserving of intellectual coverage, but I do not know how many are currently under investigation.

Commendable efforts are already taking place throughout the globe in such countries as the USA, the European Union and other countries of the Organization of Economic Co-operation and Development. A prime example is provided by the leadership of the International Telecommunications Union (Touré, 2011).

- **Same or different:** Is cyber warfare different from orthodox or classic warfare? Or is it – even if apparently "non-violent" – just a form of war, adapted to the conditions of contemporary society? Does it require special actions to combat it? What are the "small" or "limited" experiences of cyber-attacks that have taken place, for example, in Estonia in 2012? Cyber attacks are being listed on a monthly basis and there is a kind of structure underpinning what is happening. Attacks are wide-ranging and global, and do not seem to discriminate among governments and companies; there is a further group of attacks that relate to damage on specific organizations; and finally there are politically motivated destructive onslaughts aimed at sabotage and espionage (cyberwarfare). One example of a destructive attack is Stuxnet, which was a malicious computer worm perceived to be been built as an American-Israeli cyber weapon. Examples of later cyberwarfare targeting government and commercial institutions are the 2010 cyberattacks on Burma, the 2013 Singapore cyberattacks by Anonymous and those related to web censorship regulations.
- **Traditional concerns transposed into modern society:** What kind of relationship exists between "attack" and "defense" in various

political systems? How do the hierarchies that exist in traditional military domains correspond to the relative lack of hierarchy that exists in cyber warfare? How much does the variability in control of the Internet influence the networks that operate across national borders (i.e., its apparent lack of centralized control or its relative freedom from control)? How do traditional hierarchies complicate these matters?

- **New fields of warfare:** Are there any comparisons to be made between attacks on countries or regions and attacks on global financial systems? What parallels are there between cyber warfare and attacks on international trade? What about attacks that are made on specific infrastructures such as utilities or energy systems? How similar to each other are the threats connected with nuclear power and those associated with cyber warfare?
- **Play versus actuality:** What relationship is there between developments in aggression/violence, violent behavior in society, and playing electronic war games and/or electronic games of extreme violence? Could an accumulated collective aggression shift towards a desire to undertake cyber-attacks? As a result, who would be defined as being guilty?
- **Speed:** What role does the speed of the accumulation of capital, information, and communications, as well as ICT in its own right, play in aggravating these developments?

These classic questions should enable an analysis by researchers working on ICT in peace and war. These five issues could become the starting point for a set of alternatives, in terms of both thinking and acting, on an individual and global scale. From my perspective, the challenge is to move these questions beyond simply the military domain and out into all other parts of society – because ICT affects all other parts of society.

4.4 A need for growth in alternative thinking and acting

A "nonviolence movement" against nonviolent cyberwarfare is needed: I think that this should be a form of grass roots movement – or network of networks – that shares the same vision of reaching the Good Information and Communication Society as I have expressed throughout this whole book.

Historically, advocates of activist philosophies of nonviolence have used a range of methods in their campaigns for social change. These methods have included critical forms of education and persuasion, civil disobedience and nonviolent direct action, and social, political, cultural and economic forms of intervention. In recent centuries, and also within the first decade of the 21st century, nonviolent methods of action have acted as powerful tools for social protest and revolutionary social and political change. For example, today people need to know how to be resilient even in the most dire and tragic circumstances (Cameron, 2011).

People in general, including academics, need to start a new movement for ICT that is used for peace, harmony, and collaboration. The latest forms of ICT can be used for constructive interaction between people, valuable dialogue, and the enrichment of human feelings and thinking.

Alongside personal, organizational, and national resilience, as a counter-movement, people need to start a new phase of activity in favor of ICT that is used for peace, harmony, and collaboration. The passive acceptance of inappropriate and ill-considered – some might even say "evil" – uses of ICT has to be prevented. If and when secure and sustainable, ICT may actually help to reduce risks.

ICT can and should be used to narrow the gap between subcultures, and to bridge the differences between different religious systems. It could, instead, show people what the similarities are among cultures, emphasize the synergies among the various cultural and faith-based blocks, and bring us all into a thrilling, fruitful dialogue with each other.

An approach which would be based on the achievement of a future "unity and diversity" in the world (Bradley et al., 2011) has to be emphasized. This would be a much more cross-disciplinary approach based on broader theoretical perspectives than in past times. It should, first, be feasible to be put into practice and, second, help all people to work on preventive action strategies.

An excellent example of such an approach was the way in which the 2011 Nobel Prize for Peace was offered to three women from different nations in Africa. That year, the Nobel Peace Prize was awarded jointly to Ellen Johnson Sirleaf, Leymah Gbowee, and Tawakkol Karman "for their non-violent struggle for the safety of women and for women's rights to full participation in peace-building work" (www.nobelprize.org/nobel_prizes/peace/laureates/2011/press.html).

Ellen Johnson Sirleaf said,

> As curtains are raised and as the sun shines upon dark places, what was previously invisible comes into view. Technology has turned our world into one interconnected neighborhood. What happens in one place is seen in every corner, and there has been no better time for the spread of peace, democracy and their attending social justice and fairness for all. Today, across the globe, women, and also men, from all walks of life are finding the courage to say, loudly and firmly, in a thousand languages, "No more." They reject mindless violence, and defend the fundamental values of democracy, of open society, of freedom, and of peace.
> (www.nobelprize.org/nobel_prizes/peace/laureates/
> 2011/johnson_sirleaf-lecture_en.html)

Often people are saying these things with the help of ICT. I think that the perspective must be "that even the most impossible must be seen as possible". Is a unified women's movement globally possible – with a direct mission to stop all wars? A men's movement needs to be based on the human right to refuse to kill other human beings.

Steps for Peace is a non-profit organization that supports social and political transformation processes in crisis regions (www.steps-for-peace.org/en/). Its work focuses on education, research, and development cooperation. In addition to training peace educators, including people who would act as mediators, the organization "provides a forum for practitioners and theorists for systematic reflection and exchange of expertise in peace work", in search of practical methods to transform societies. In this context, I would like to cite Åke Hassbjer of Steps for Peace, who says that "religions are splitting people up – faith is unifying people". I would note that violent wars and aggression in world history have roots in religious, economic, and personal lust for power. The Crusaders killed people of other faiths in order to change peoples' religions to their own. Some of the terrorists today argue that they are sent by God to make all people "right-minded".

Religions have often been used by political and economic forces, but religious institutions can also respond to provide us with a safe future on Earth. For example, in Sweden, most churches are pretty empty these days, except for special occasions such as Christmases, weddings, and funerals. However, recently, a church near my own home has shifted its focus to work more on climate change issues. I find this interesting.

In the end, I would also circle back to my call to individual responsibility: all people on Earth, the believers as well as the agnostics, have to collaborate. That collaboration must be in the spirit of love, responsibility, and truth. It will take all sorts of organizations to make this happen.

4.5 Constructive suggestions

Here, then, are some initial thoughts on a variety of tools that can be used, in particular, to prevent and fight cyber warfare. A brainstorming exercise under the framework of the IADIS July 2011 conference (Bradley et al., 2011) highlighted the formulation of an initial set of possible positive positions and tools. These tools related principally to four domains. The domains were awareness-building; education and development; software and games; and seeing the issues from an international perspective. There is no particular prioritization in the order of the issues below. All are important and would benefit from further investigation and, moreover, immediate action.

In terms of *awareness-building*, it is important not just to increase the consciousness of the threats of cyber warfare, but also to:

• Create an understanding of how contemporary society is built and what are its underpinnings, invisible infrastructures (for example, based on

the economy, electricity, transportation, and water). From this under-standing, an awareness of the counterbalancing vulnerability of society needs to be built.
- Create the potential for positive, new uses of ICT. The 2011 IADIS ICT, Society and Human Beings conference (Bradley et al., 2011), for example, dealt with many examples of ICT use that can help to make people aware of what can be done to combat global warming; what can be done ecologically and environmentally in a positive way; how to help people who are at the bottom of the pyramid in society; how to enhance the lives of both the very young and especially also the very elderly; and how to use ICT in health, welfare, and well-being.
- Work together to create space and time for constructive discussion and debate in forums and *agora*, as much physically and in real-time as in cyberspace and on the Internet.
- Use cyberspace for dialogue and for the search for the common essence of all faiths, religions, and philosophical and spiritual endeavors.
- Hold dialogues about common value systems. Again, for example, in the 2011 IADIS ICT, Society and Human Beings conference several inspi-rational panels were held on human rights and on "unity and diversity".

In terms of *education and development*, ICT is employed directly and indi-rectly to:

- Examine the experience of early childhood in relation to ICT and the influence of ICT on childhood and adult development. In this respect, the pedagogical work of Maria Montessori, and schools which follow in the tradition of her thinking, is of especial importance. The cele-brated Italian physician devoted her life to developing a learning phi-losophy for children that has become widespread internationally. Her approach became a hot issue before, during and after the Second World War. One of her books dealt especially with education and peace.
- Explore strategies to encourage human and humane roles instead of further strengthening traditional "male" and "female" roles. Emancipa-tion is needed for men and women, boys and girls. Until now, emanci-pation has focused largely on what is meant by it for women.
- Emphasize an assessment of ICT's influence on boys and men because it is so much more often the male gender that wages war. While all of us are the victims of warfare, war often particularly affects women and children.
- Consider education more and more in the context of global learning.
- Ensure that global and international trade shifts instead towards, and includes, a "Global and International Educational System".
- Explore the potential for "commoning" (sharing) in the ICT society. Karin Bradley describes in books, articles, and a documentary film how the process of commoning is growing in increasing fields, due

to future lack of natural resources and also depict a future of sharing economy beyond capitalism as well as socialism. She draws examples from the computer world like Wikipedia where all can contribute, thereby challenging the historical concept of ownership (Bradley, K., 2014).

In terms of *software and electronic games,* ICT is employed directly and indirectly to:

• Begin to use multimedia products in a positive peace-oriented way.
• Focus on developing "peace games" across cultures and religions.
• Develop a role and purpose for anti-war games.
• Stop developing games based on extreme violence.

From an *international perspective,* ICT is employed directly and indirectly to:

• Stop the automation (occasionally called the "robotization") of international, economic transactions that involve an increase in the risk of conflict development. Iordanis Kavathatzopoulos drew attention to this sensitive area with regard to automating decision-making in relation to robots at his presentation at the conference Human Choice and Computers (HCC11) in 2014.
• Robotization and Ethics need a public debate. Robotization has been around for long time in industry, and is now a growing and dynamic area. A lot of uses within the service sector, for example, for health tracking, surgery, and elder care and in the home are being developed and on the focus for research and development. Definite ethical attention at an early stage is needed so that a humane goal becomes reality.
• Rethink the current trends that are occurring regarding the development and use of humanlike robots.
• Explore the power of good examples, for example, from among Nobel Peace Prize winners. Over the more than one hundred years since the prize was first awarded, there have been fewer than ten women who have received it. Many more have been nominated.
• Explore what kinds of wise, preventative actions formal international bodies, could take, and compare these with disarmament campaigns.
• Re-think the basis of formal international bodies based on the character of today's and tomorrow's threats.
• Explore the collaboration potential between formal bodies and informal organizations, bodies and networks. Examine how the work and relationships between the non-governmental organizations, bodies and informal networks operating in the field of peace-building could be coordinated and strengthened.

- Explore specifically what particular organizations – one is IFIP – could begin to do about these challenges.
- Investigate use of social media. Social media provide quite new and powerful channels for revolts and movements for liberation and/or terrorism. More knowledge is needed to strengthen the liberation power connected to social media, for example, studies on what happened "afterwards" and what "preventive actions" are possible.

4.6 Emerging suggestions

This approach may provide a helpful set of possibilities for those networks, organizations, and institutions that are already working in this field of activity or may go on to do so in the future.

There are some phenomenal tools available to help build a Good Information and Communication Society. That society starts within ourselves and with ourselves, and the networks of which we are members. It also relates to civil society as a whole and the formal organizations that function in society.

All people have a responsibility, in their roles as researchers, policy-makers, citizens, and human beings, to consider how to leave after themselves a society in which human rights and peace form the essential elements. Stakeholders, along with ICT experts, can help society to start to answer a vast number of important questions pertaining to its potential turnaround in a positive direction.

A set of fundamental points are immediately evident:

> *Never before in history has there been such a great opportunity for peace. Let us build on that opportunity! Rethinking is required to deal with today's global problems, and transparent, rapid action too is needed. Visionary strategic tools are needed to help transform dictatorships into democracies, and to overcome not only present conflicts but also future risks.*

ICT should help people to appreciate diversity. I have been known to say that when we design, work with, and use these technologies, the focus should be on "ICT for deepening human and societal qualities" (Bradley, 2001, 2006). A major re-thinking is needed to deal with today's problems. Transparent, rapid action is needed. Let us act on it!

4.7 Acknowledgements

This chapter is based on a chapter originally written by Gunilla Bradley and Diane Whitehouse that was published in a Springer-Verlag book on

ICT infrastructures: G. Bradley and D. Whitehouse, "Challenges to Peace in the 21st Century: Working Towards a Good Information and Communication Society", in M.D. Hercheui, D. Whitehouse, W.J. McIver Jnr. & J. Phahlamohlaka (eds), *ICT, Critical Infrastructures and Society* (Heidelberg and Berlin: Springer-Verlag, 2012, pp. 274–284). The original authors were especially grateful to Jackie Phahlamohlaka, former Chair of IFIP's Technical Committee 9 on ICT and Society, who chaired a panel on peace and war at the 2011 IADIS ICT, Society and Human Beings conference in Rome, Italy, in July 2011 at which a very preliminary version of the reflection paper was first presented. They also wished to thank Willny Bradley who assisted with background desk research, and Marc Griffiths and several anonymous reviewers for their careful, constructive criticism and commentary.

Note

IFIP is a non-governmental organization that was established in 1960 under the auspices of UNESCO, IFIP. It links some 50 national and international societies and academies of science with a total membership of over half a million professionals. Activities are coordinated by 13 Technical Committees. The IFIP Technical Committee on ICT and Society was formed in 1976 to develop greater understanding of how ICT innovation is associated with changes in society and to influence the shaping of socially responsible and ethical policies and professional practices. The latest working group established in this technical committee is "ICT Uses in Peace and War".

Bibliography

Ball, K. and Webster, F. (eds.). (2003). *The Intensification of Surveillance: Crime, Terrorism and Warfare in the Information Era*. London: Pluto Press.

Berleur, J., Beardon, C. and Laufer, R. (eds.). (1993). Facing the Challenge of Risk and Vulnerability in an Information Society. Proceedings of the IFIP WG9.2 Working Conference on Facing the Challenge of Risk and Vulnerability in an Information Society, Namur, Belgium, 20–22 May.

Bjurner, A. and Wallensteen, P. (2014). *Regional Organizations in Peacemaking: Challengers to the UN?* London: Routledge.

Bradley, G. (ed.). (2001). *Humans on the Net: Information and Communication Technology (ICT) Work Organization and Human Beings*. Stockholm, Sweden: Prevent.

Bradley, G. (2006). *Social and Community Informatics – Humans on the Net*. London: Routledge.

Bradley, G., Whitehouse, D. and Singh, G. (2011). Proceedings of the IADIS International Conferences ICT, Society and Human Beings 2011 and e-Democracy, Equity and Social Justice 2011. Part of the IADIS Multi-Conference on Computer Science and Information Systems 2011. IADIS Press.

Bradley, K. (2014). Towards a peer economy – How open source and peer-to-peer architecture, hardware and consumption are transforming the economy. In Bradley, K. & Hedrén, J. (eds.), *Green utopianism – Perspectives, politics and micropractices*. New York: Routledge.

Cameron, J. (2011). A Survival Kit for Resilient Citizens in the Information Society. Presentation Made at the IFIP WG9.2 & WG 9.9 Joint Workshop, Milan, Social Accountability & Sustainability in the Information Society: Perspectives on Long-Term Responsibility, 4–5 June 2011.

Doyle, M.W. and Sambrinis, N. (2006). *Making War and Building Peace: United Nations Peace Operations*. Princeton, NJ: Princeton University Press.

Economist, The. (2010). The War in the Fifth Domain: Are the Mouse and the Keyboard the New Weapons of Conflict? July 1 2010. www.economist.com/node/16478792, accessed 19 July 2014.

European Commission. (2012). *Tackling Crime in Our Digital Age: Establishing a European Cybercrime Centre*. Brussels: European Commission. 28.03.2012. COM (2012) 140 Final. http://ec.europa.eu/home-affairs/doc_centre/crime/docs/Communication%20-%20European%20Cybercrime%20Centre.pdf, accessed 19 July 2014.

Höglund, K. and Fjelde, H. (eds). (2011). *Building Peace, Creating Conflict: Conflictual Dimensions of Local and International Peacebuilding*. Lund, Sweden: Nordic Academic Press.

Kajtazi, M. (2012). An Exploration of Information Inadequacy: The Lack of Needed Information in Human, Social and Industrial Affairs. In: Hercheui, M., Whitehouse, D., Phahlamohlaka, and McIver, W.J., Jr (eds.), *ICT Critical Infrastructures and Society: IFIP Advances in Information and Communication Technology*. Berlin/Heidelberg, Germany: Springer-Verlag.

Kavathatzopoulos, I. (2014). Independent Agents and Ethics. In: Kimppa, K., Whitehouse, D., Kuusela, T., and Phahlamohlaka, J. (eds.), *ICT and Society: Advances in Information and Communication Technology*. Berlin/Heidelberg: Springer, 39–46.

Konrath, S. H., O'Brien, E. H. and Hsing, C. (2011). Changes in Dispositional Empathy in American College Students Over Time: A Meta-Analysis. *Personality and Social Psychology*, 15 (2), 80–198.

Kuhn, T. S. (1962). *The Structure of Scientific Revolutions*. Chicago: University of Chicago Press.

Livingstone, S. (2014). In Their Own Words: What Bothers Children Online? *European Journal of Communication*, June, 29, 271–288, first published on March 3, 2014.

Livingstone, S., Haddon, L., Görzig, A. and Ólafsson, K. (2011). *Risks and Safety on the Internet: The Perspective of European Children: Full Findings and Policy Implications from the EU Kids Online Survey of 9–16 Year Olds and Their Parents in 25 Countries*. London, UK: EU Kids Online, Deliverable D4. EU Kids Online Network.

Olsson, A., Petrovic, P. and Ingvar, M. (2012). *Så ska EU stoppa cyberbrotten*. DN Debate.

SvD Opinion. (2012). Så ska EU stoppa cyberbrotten. 28 March 2012. www.svd.se/opinion/brannpunkt/sa-ska-eu-stoppa-cyberbrotten_6957681.svd, accessed 19 July 2014.

Swedish Media Council. (2011). *The Violent Computer Games and Aggression – an Overview of the Research 2000–2011*. Swedish Media Council. www.statensmediierad.se, accessed 19 July 2014.

Touré, H.I. (2011). *The Quest for Cyber Peace*. Geneva, Switzerland: International Telecommunications Union.

UCDP (The Uppsala Conflict Data Program) offers a number of datasets on organized violence and peacemaking, most of which are updated on an annual basis. http://ucdp.uu.se or directly http://ucdp.uu.se/downloads. The UCDP Conflict Encyclopedia (UCDP database) is an online, free of charge, database containing detailed descriptive information on armed conflicts, peace agreements, and several other aspects of organized violence. Coverage is global with information from 1946 and onwards.

Uppsala Center for Peace Research Info. www.pcr.uu.se/about/news_archive/2015, accessed 31 December 2015.

Wallensteen, P. (2015). *Quality Peace: Peacebuilding, Victory and World Order*. Oxford: Oxford University Press.

Whitehouse, D. (2012). Benchmarking eHealth in the European Union. Presentation Made at the IFIP WG9.2 Workshop on, ICT Critical Infrastructure and Social Accountability: Methods, Tools and Techniques. London, 4 February 2012.

Whitehouse, D., Hilty, L., Patrignani, N. and Lieshout, M. van. (2011). Introduction. In: Whitehouse, D., Hilty, L., Patrignani, N., and Lieshout, M. van (eds.), *Social Accountability and Sustainability in the Information Society: Perspectives in Long-Term Responsibility*. Rome: Notizie di Politeia, 3–12.

Zaki J., and Ochsner, K. (2012). The neuroscience of empathy: progress, pitfalls and promise. *Nature Neuroscience* 15, 675–680.

Zartmann, W. (2004). Pronouncement at Event Entitled Civil War: Need, Creed and Greed. October 21, 2004. www.cgdev.org/content/calendar/detail/3019/, accessed 19 July 2014.

5 Voices from around the world on quality of life and well-being in the ICT society

- Background to the survey
- Questions about the self and daily life
- Questions about life in general, human life, and people's lives
- Aspects regarded as the most positive and most negative with regard to ICT
- Direct quotes from respondents
- Some interviews in 2016
- Interviewing myself in 2013
- My answers in 2016

Dear Reader,

Please take a cup of tea or coffee or make yourself a smoothie, and spend some time thinking about the seven questions that follow. A little space is provided after each question for your answers, but you might want to use a notebook and write down your answers separately. Then you can revisit the questions again, after reading this book, or even after reading the rest of this chapter, in which I will share with you my and others' answers. You may even want to revisit these questions sometime in the near future, to see how your answers have changed.

The questions are related to *the convergence model* described in Chapter 3. They cover the four clusters of circles which represent the life environment, life role, globalization, and ICT. The questions focus primarily on the middle of the model – the sunflower – which is the impact of ICT on human beings.

What is quality of life for you?

. . .

What impact has ICT had on quality of life (e.g., personal computers, laptops, smart phones) in general?

. . .

What are the positive things or advantages of ICT?

...

What are the negative things or disadvantages of ICT?

...

What observations and reflections do you have about people's lives
in the ICT society?

...

What are the good things?

...

What are the bad things?

...

Now, please take a look at how other people around the globe responded
to these same questions.

5.1 Background to the survey

In January 2013, my colleague Diane Whitehouse and I recognized that new
calendar years are good moments to reflect on one's own life and life in
general. We wanted to draw on the insights of a group of fellow thinkers and
scholars, friends and acquaintances. Our 18 respondents have a wide range
of research, teaching, and consultancy jobs, and they came from Belgium,
Brazil, Italy, Poland, Sweden, the UK, and the USA. They were of various
ages and both genders.

We asked our respondents to complete our questionnaire in much the
same way that I have introduced it to you here. Since we did not wish to
constrain their writing or thinking, we asked them to feel free to interpret
our questions as they wished. They could just answer the questions that
were on issues that were the most meaningful for them. Their answers could
be as brief or as lengthy as they wanted, and they could reply to as many
questions as suited them. Mostly, our respondents answered the entire set
of questions. This is a study that has so far been unpublished and was a personal endeavour, but was conducted with a social research structure.

Gunnar Myrdal, a Swedish Nobel laureate, economist, sociologist, and
politician, has argued that there is no value-free research. In this sense, we
have explored – with other thinkers and scholars, friends and acquaintances –
a topic of importance to ourselves and to them. The answers and interpreta-
tions are a mirror of who we are and who they are. In terms of methodology,
the full answers to the questions in the finalized interview guide were first
brought together in a long, rich, textual document. A qualitative analysis

was then undertaken to extract patterns and find keywords with similar content – using colored pencils and a "cut-and-paste" technique. Sometimes the answers have been grouped together as positive, negative, and/ or neutral responses. This terminology reflects our own analysis, and was not specified in the questions posed. The full answers have helped to validate this overall classification. In the compact description that follows, bold text highlights some preliminary conclusions from these 2013 interviews. Elsewhere, italicized text emphasizes some important points. While most responses are summarized here, I include some direct quotes. Actual quotations are identified by the use of quotation marks; these are anonymized, though I have included a brief description of some of our respondents.

Following the in-depth exploration of the survey responses, I then continue by recounting a further set of interviews done with colleagues, friends, family, and even myself, from 2013 and 2016.

5.2 Questions about the self and daily life

5.2.1 ICT and changes in people's life

In the first half of the survey, the focus was on the changes taking place in people's own lives as a result of ICT being introduced into their daily lives; the most positive aspects, and the most negative aspects; and what the quality of life or a good life means to them.

People's answers were mainly positive, but some of their answers were negative or broadly neutral.

Positively

Communications are *easier*; ICT changed people's lives a lot, people said. In some cases, ICT *drastically* changed life, making it hard to find a balance. Some responded that their *self-esteem* had increased. One respondent said that ICT "enhanced my life and supported my learning to learn." ICT has led to more *collectivism* and has a huge implication for *civic intelligence*. But the real big change in life is the "smart phone" more than anything else.

Negatively

The challenges that were brought up by our respondents concerned "system complexity especially with humans" and that life had become more "fragmented" especially regarding relationships.

Neutral

Some expressed a *more balanced view* listing some positive and some negative things. Some were sceptical of the claims of the benefits of new electronic

devices with a tension between the pleasures of availability of credible information but were depressed by what they called "a lot of nonsense".

5.2.2 Most positive aspects or disadvantages?

The key positive issues perceived were accessibility; the enabling, enriching, and facilitating of life; the possibilities offered by speed; and, last but
not least, the opportunities offered for the environment.

The dominant word regarding positive change was **access**. There was
a clear enthusiasm about the new opportunity of having access, with
mention of human knowledge; connection to family; and having friends
even in foreign countries. Other aspects of access were finding a partner
for work or personal relationship; getting access to institutions; and getting financial information. Other areas mentioned were access to books
and articles; news; services for entertainment, education, and health
information.

Some emphasized and qualified the word "access" by referring to the
enabling, enriching, and facilitating of life. More seldom "access independent of physical distance" was mentioned. Some people highlighted the
great opportunity for **independence** offered by technologies – you do not
need to ask other people for certain things.

More indirectly, the issue of **speed** was expressed by using such words
as fast, immediately, swiftly, and easy. Finally one person mentioned the
positive potential for the **environment** due to the reduction in travelling.

People are continuously becoming more used to, and take for granted,
having access to information and being able to communicate with people
and institutions independent of time and space. They sometimes take for
granted having access to that fast connection anytime and anywhere.

Maybe the increasing access to information and to people that ICT provides is in the long run increasing our desire to explore experiences in real
life [IRL] and to meet people face-to-face in order to enrich ourselves. Is
this an approach a better quality of life here? One respondent addressed
sustainability, meaning that people now have to make choices that have
long-lasting impact on the material circumstances of the future.

5.3.3 Most negative aspects or disadvantages?

Most interviewees mentioned **a loss of important qualities in human
beings, and the interactions between humans**. This seems to be the case
in spite of all the aforementioned positive things. I list some key responses
from the interviews:

- A distance between human beings
- Decline in quality, reliability, and trustworthiness of content

- Identity problems
- Fraudsters
- Vulnerability of young and old people
- Difficulties for children in handling smart phones
- Addictiveness
- Negative influence of smart phones for all aspects of life
- Hard for children
- Violence and children's behaviour. Confusion between the virtual and the real world

Many items that were mentioned about the confusion between virtual reality [VR] and real life [RL] refer to people at different parts of the life cycle, i.e., the very young and young and the old and very old. For many years "addictiveness and games" has been a problem that has been discussed, linked with anxiety. Looking around today, it seems like most of us are "addicted" to the mobiles in our pockets or bags that are becoming smarter and smarter. Just look around at the airport, at public spaces, at restaurants. We could ask ourselves: What do we win? What do we lose? What are the short- and long-term impacts? Is there a way back to some of the things we have lost?

The other group of responses concerned various aspects of **stress** due to the increase in diversity of goods, services, and information. These are the words used by the respondents:

- It takes too much time to make a choice (the tyranny of freedom of options?)
- Exhausting and time-consuming
- Distracting
- Hard to focus on essentials
- Less time for silence, meditation, and deep interactions. Loss of liberty due to the perceived pressure to react rapidly to emails

I think that it would be of value to explore how various cultures and religious systems might handle this societal transition. Do the words used by the respondents mirror the situation in Western cultures? I have met enthusiasm in countries where there was a leap into the use of mobile equipment without people having to go the long way round through dependencies on an old infrastructure. Gaps between rural and urban areas have been overcome by access to mobile phones. However, the long-term effects are hard to foresee and will probably ultimately become similar around the world.

5.3.4 *What does quality of life (or "a good life") mean for* you *and what contributes most to a good quality of life for* you?

Some people summarized their responses in an **all-encompassing way**, by mentioning several real-life aspects of the quality of life. The following are the words used by three respondents:

- Healthy food; well-constructed shelter; robust physical health; close, trusted, and trusting friends; reliable, clean public transportation; reliable, reputable sources of news and information; structured educational materials (for use in teaching or self-improvement); an open, tolerant mind; patience; a range of useful, demanding, rewarding activities (to oneself and to others); time to reflect.
- Sustainable environment, possibility for creative work for all, common ownership and control of the economy, participatory democracy, and an integrative culture that enables learning and social interaction of all.
- Feeling secure, having a home, loved ones, family, friends, not fearing to lose basic functions as a stable home, food, and amenities for you and your family. Living in a society that is equal, democratic, and open, where all are treated with respect and have good living conditions.

Others focused on aspects of **freedom**: for example, being able to do what they want and when.

Others mentioned some **specific issues** like having a job; earning enough money; being healthy; when a doctor's help is needed, receiving it immediately; having access to the Internet and phone. Having a **good work-life balance** was often mentioned.

A few people mentioned some more **psychosocial and philosophical aspects** such as:

- Continuously learning things and enjoying a proper balance and *enjoying all the senses* of our bodies.
- Assuming that the basics such as food, shelter, and good health are in place; *active engagement* in something that benefits others; opportunities for physical exercise and the enjoyment of nature; time for reflection.
- Not fearing to lose basic functions as a stable home, food, and amenities for you and your family. Living in a society that is *equal, democratic, and open*, where all are treated with respect and have good living conditions.
- A sense of community; an interesting job that provide *contributions to the community* and the environment; a lifestyle with a low environmental impact.

- Family and friends are a given I assume: Talking and thinking about *"real" issues and trying to do something* about them, creative projects, engage with people – seeing art, theatre, etc., walking and wandering around.
- *Peace and freedom* assumed; easy access to intellectual and cultural richness, having numerous friends, *quietness and beauty* of nature.
- Trying to *spread happiness* and joy around which repays it tenfold.
- *Four factors that interact*: ecology, economy, politics, and culture.

I think that, in general, the main aspects for having a good life and quality of life concern very basic social factors related to interplay between humans. It seems to be important to reflect where technology has taken us and where we want to go from now. This is also emphasized when we look at the factors (aspects) which are regarded as the most positive things related to ICT (see section 5.4 below).

5.3 Questions about life in general, human life, and people's lives

With more general questions at the end of the survey, we wanted to get at the broader view. We wanted to know what our respondents thought about the quality of life at a societal level, and the impacts from ICT in general.

5.3.1 Impact on people's quality of life

The first question was phrased as follows **"What impact on the quality of life in society has ICT had in general?"** Below is the main content in the answers listed in short paragraphs – sometimes shortened a little without interfering with their meanings.

- *Speeding up* things.
- Made us *more independent* but on the other hand *more dependent*, addicted, closed, and more concentrated on ourselves.
- *Quality of work life* has improved for people who with ease understand/ use new technologies. For other people struggling with the new technology is a hindering factor for qualitative work. Enables result-driven project work; for *private life* it also depends – people with distant family relations they can communicate easier. For others living nearby friends, it creates an unnecessary distraction/ barrier.
- ICT is enabling to people with disabilities, and to those without access to certain services. Disabling – ICT can remove the need to leave one's home at all. ICT can simultaneously broaden and reduce the gaps between the haves and have-nots.
- Four realms of human existence – ecology, economy, politics, and culture – had antagonistic realities – both very positive potentials and huge risks.

- ICT has perhaps democratized access to information and the possibility to spread their ideas, organize things, trade things outside the big corporate markets.
- Taken together, ICT has not contributed to improved quality of life, often generated more stress, distraction, concentration difficulties, obesity, feeling of being constant competitors.
- Children can learn how to use advanced information visualization tools for producing digital content.
- Very controversial; in general positive, but some negative impacts without a "wise" development and use of technologies.

5.3.2 Characterizing people's lives

The second question was phrased as follows *"How would you characterize the present era and people's lives with regard to society and technology"?* Below is the main content in the answers listed – sometimes a little shortened without, however, interfering with the meaning, hence these sentences are very close to direct quotes.

- Increased interest in the material things in life, along with a fantasy world of gaming and wanting stuff.
- We live faster. We are more stressed, because due to mobile phones and the Internet, work is more present in our private life. As a result, it is difficult to relax. The way of communication has changed too. On one hand, it is easier to communicate with people living far from us, but we also have less time for people whom earlier we met directly.
- People who have fully embraced and are active on social media networks are maybe enjoying life, but it seems to me no longer to be really present in real-life. Social media is kind of a distraction, like gaming.
- People are stressed.
- For some, a richer and deeper phenomenon with more channels to communicate with a greater number of people. For others, society is a more invasive, undesirable approach from organizations and individuals.
- We do not understand all of the implications of the continued development and spread of ICT: we cannot see all of the treasures in Aladdin's cave, or all of the demons in Pandora's Box.
- ICT has the ability to extend our cognitive and communicative capabilities. However, some suspicion and circumspection will yield to the desire to use the technology.
- I think first and foremost we live in a capitalist society, in which the accumulation of money, power, and status stratifies the lives of people and creates a class society. ICT is embedded into these structures of inequality.

- ICT has perhaps democratized access to information and also the possibility for people to express and spread their ideas through blogs, social media, online magazines, etc. It has made it easier to organize things, to swap and trade things outside the big corporate markets.
- Stimulating human beings, enhancing their knowledge.
- "Product for a market" and not for improving our "well-being".
- Taken together, however, I think much of ICT has not contributed to improved quality of life; I think it has often generated more stress, distraction, concentration difficulties, obesity, and a feeling of being constant competitors.

5.4 Aspects regarded as the most positive and most negative with regard to ICT

5.4.1 The most positive aspects of ICT

The main positive aspects of ICT mentioned by our respondents are the **opportunity it offers of sharing**, **cooperating**, **communicating with people**, and **social relations**. They expressed these aspects as follows:

- Sharing expertise/know-how/views
- More sharing, cooperation, and social relations and points towards a new type of society that goes beyond capitalism
- Enabled peer-to-peer trading
- Open source movement and that individuals can create their own digital content/simulations understanding diverse sciences concepts
- "Being in contact" at a global scale

The main other group of answers relate to **work** and **education** more directly. These answers were expressed as follows:

- Work at a distance
- Mobility in work
- More possibilities of education
- More and better knowledge, all is small, smart, light, facilitating life with mobile equipment
- The possibility of getting access to articles, finding images.
- Ease of communications
- Possibility of increased equality and institutional transparency
- The most positive aspects are the opportunities for sharing knowledge, memories, and stories among human beings

Some people mentioned institutional **transparency** and **equality**.

5.4.2 *The most negative aspects of ICT*

Three sets of negative items were mentioned by our respondents. They referred to the loss of human and societal qualities, stress, and the risk of larger societal struggles.

The main negative aspects are **a loss of human and societal qualities**. This was expressed in various terms as:

- Vulnerability. The immense centralized storage of information and data in the "cloud" is "scary".
- Addiction to the Internet and mobile phones
- Cheating and theft
- Interference with privacy
- Not using our bodies any more (becoming unhealthy)
- Risks of reduced equality and transparency
- Facebook and smart phones are transforming others around us – people are not being present in Real Life [RL]
- Children and smart phones – their relationship is difficult
- Quality of life is challenged by smart phones

The other main group of answers relates to various forms of **stress**.

- Distraction; loss of attention to essentials
- Stress due to too much acceleration to individuals' thinking and behaviour
- Compression of time – always "on"

Finally, growing commercialization, the exploitation of labour, and the risk of societal **struggles** were mentioned.

5.5 Direct quotes from respondents

In this last section of the chapter, we have selected just a few quotations from people who have quite different backgrounds. We present the items that they mentioned as being either the most positive aspect or advantage of ICT or the three most important factors that contribute to a good quality of life.

Despite the cultural and gender differences in the respondents, many of the positives they mentioned have to do with the general ease of communication either with professional and work colleagues, or with family and friends, or both. Depending on their age and competences, the respondents had the capacity or not to compare and contrast these developments over time – and often over quite a considerable number of decades.

Several respondents mentioned the benefits arising from particular types of applications. The benefits range from the creation of content to greater access to services related to health, education, and entertainment. Given the professional interest that some of the respondents have in the domain of ICT and Society, it is not surprising that in some cases they also mentioned general societal trends. Their quotations end with the balanced viewpoint that, despite polarities, positive social change is feasible.

5.5.1   What are the most positive aspects or advantages of ICT?

A BUSINESSWOMAN FROM SWEDEN: "Positives are mostly related to my professional role, and negative aspects to my private role. For the professional role, I think [technology] allows a tremendous opportunity to be an independent worker and to connect to people around the globe. My business (supporting companies' expansion process to new markets) is 100% driven by use of new technology: for example, we use cloud-based tools such as High-rise (www.highrisehq.com, accessed 26 August 2015), social media like LinkedIn (http://gb.linkedin.com, accessed 26 August 2015), and storage facilities like Dropbox (www. dropbox.com, accessed 26 August 2015) to enable business and projects. Mobility is key to working anywhere at any time."

AN E-GOVERNMENT EXPERT: "Ease of communications while equipment and networks [are] operating – panic when they fail."

A WOMAN WHO IS BLIND: "Access to a big quantity of books . . . independence in writing documents and e-mails, with no control of a sighted person. Due to mobile phones, easier and more safe travels and, to [the] speaking programme installed on my mobile, independence in writing and reading SMSs."

A WOMAN FROM BELGIUM: "The possibility to communicate with my relatives even when they are abroad, but also the opportunity to reach immediately the specialist in my field of research."

A RETIRED WOMAN FROM SWEDEN: "For me, to be able to keep in touch with family and friends by e-mail wherever they are globally. To conduct research without having to sit in libraries and copy text by hand. Not least to feel that I am keeping up with my grandchildren and not being left behind!"

A MEDIA TECHNOLOGY PROFESSOR: "I think the most positive aspects of networked computing [are] that it socializes production, knowledge, [and] labour – all of this now involves more sharing, cooperation and social relations, and points towards a new type of society that goes beyond capitalism."

A TEACHER IN HIS LATE 30S FROM BRAZIL: "The low cost is related to the growing accessibility to web-based information and visualization technologies that have supported opportunities [for] ordinary individuals' appropriation of digital tools and techniques for creating content . . . In general, technology has . . . created lots of e-services that have allowed an increase in individuals' accessibility, for instance, to health, entertainment and education services."

A SCIENTIST FROM THE USA: "I'm neither an optimist nor a pessimist, as both viewpoints assume a natural or inevitable gravitation towards one extreme or the other. [I have] a belief that positive social change is possible and that people can play a role."

5.5.2 *What are the most important factors that contribute to a good quality of life for you?*

It is interesting, and revealing, to note the seriousness and basic character of those factors that our respondents mentioned in terms of the factors that can offer a good quality of life: they are often the fundamentals of Maslow's hierarchy of needs. They relate, for example, to physiology, safety, and love or belonging. They are not at all related to self-actualization or self-fulfilment.

A CANADIAN MAN: "Assuming that the basics such as food, shelter, and good health are in place: active engagement in something that benefits others; opportunities for physical exercise and the enjoyment of nature; time for reflection."

A SWEDISH RESEARCHER: "Feeling secure, having a home, loved ones, family, friends, not fearing to lose [such] basic functions as a stable home, food and amenities for you and your family. Living in a society that is equal, democratic, and open, where all are treated with respect and have good living conditions."

A DOCTORAL STUDENT FROM BRAZIL: "Have access to natural resources; learning to respect [those resources]; have a peaceful place to live."

AN ITALIAN MAN: "A collection of friends, loved ones and a sense of community; an interesting job that could provide contributions to the community and to the environment; a lifestyle with a low environmental impact."

5.6 Some interviews in 2016

In November 2015, I spent a few days in the mountains of Mallorca for a writing workshop – about 10 people were gathered together, trying to write down our memories over some days of relaxation and reflections. This brought me the opportunity to ask these new friends to respond to my questions and, after a few weeks, in 2016 I received their answers. I deliberately spoke with people who either are very involved with the topic of ICT and society in their working lives or else have worked with children. These written interviews can be seen as complementary, but different, to the earlier survey responses, and can also be read as more in-depth and thoughtful replies. Time and speed of the technological development do impact.

My feelings are that, as time goes by, people are adapting to ICT and also changing focus due to their own passage in life and due to what is mainly being discussed in the mass media at the time. People's perceptions at the present time are often also related to the use of new applications of ICT. During the past few years ICT has mainly been thought of as being the Internet, perhaps with some hardware thrown in, such as mobile smart phones, or the adoption of laptops and iPads and other devices.

5.6.1 Interview with an employee working for the European Commission

What does quality of life (or "a good life") mean for you?

"For the sake of condensation I only briefly mention all the negative-side aspects (no war, no genocide, no famine, no natural catastrophes or deadly diagnoses directly affecting my family, at least for a long time to come). I understand the question as What do I appreciate most in life barring extremes, negatives as well as sudden huge wealth from a lottery (the latter often a mixed blessing).

Feel I have grown through the phase in life when technical improvement, car, hifi, TV made one satisfied and enthusiastic for a while. I don't say this is a sign of maturity or intellectual snobbery. There are folks who upgrade (change) their motorcycle every three years and seem to be in the best of moods all the time and talk about little else to other people, and I can feel a certain envy.

I feel the happiest when I sense I have at least a relatively good margin to choose when I want to spend time with people around me, my family or sometimes other friends, but also to have the right to withdraw with my own thoughts and writings. To be at least halfway understood if I say that I spent two hours reflecting over a certain, say historical event, or discussed it with a friend, no 'solution' came out of it, nothing was written down or let alone led to any income, and the terrace could have been cleaned of leaves and sand during the same two hours, which is a visible result (if not permanent, there will be new leaves tomorrow), but that there are people around seeing that the discussion about why world leaders couldn't rest on the trigger in 1914 can be just as valuable for us as humans, even if it is a drop in the ocean compared to all the bookshelf miles already written on the subject by specialists. Think, write, enjoy music, preferably in company."

What impact on the quality of life in society has ICT had in general?

"I referred to being left in peace, which has become more difficult with ICT. The email is a double-edged sword. I believe we often feel that the email we're about to write, with enclosures and links and everything requiring 20 minutes to read, is extra relevant, brilliant, funny or urgent. To the receiver it is one out of, say, 70 emails received that day. The sender with the extra urgent and relevant message is anxiously awaiting a reaction, and the receiver has got a bad conscience for not having the time to do so, or is simply indifferent or even irritated. Likewise the mobile phone is a magic tool when we WANT to tell people where we are and when we will arrive, but that incoming signal is a nuisance when we DON'T."

How would you characterize the present era and people's lives with regard to society and technology?

"The generation having grown up with ICT, such as my sons, see enormous advantages, as they know how to error-search the system when something goes wrong and find alternative solutions, they do homework together online – speaking for free via Skype, search information more easily, plus all the gaming and streaming entertainment aspects. One could argue that they therefore meet less face to face, but in a large relatively dangerous city such as where I live, especially if you're a blond Nordic boy who may carry an expensive smartphone on you, I sometimes prefer that they help out with homework via Skype rather than taking public transport late in the evening. Personally I most appreciate quick information search via the Internet and the possibility to stream music and already broadcast TV shows whenever I want, often at no extra cost. Otherwise I have enough screen time in my office.

"A society where corporations, banks, postal services, authorities, public transport systems develop in a direction where you HAVE to own a smartphone or a special tool for most transactions is going to exclude people, especially elderly people, who have no wish to install computers at home and little experience of how to handle them. Soon Aunt Aina, aged 83, will never go to concerts anymore because it is too complicated to buy at ticket (she needs a Visa number, a token, a code) or to buy an airline ticket or even travel by tram".

What opportunities are there for society and societal development as a result of ICT?

"I cannot claim to have an insight in all fields of industrial design and rationalization, but computers have already radically improved efficiency and results in many professional fields, not least in the shape of medical technologies for analysis, computer-assisted surgery, intelligent prostheses, tools for disabled people to read and write, and much more that would not have been possible earlier".

What risks are there for society and societal development as a result of ICT?

"Apart from the above unintended consequences, there is of course deliberate criminal activity such as hacking and distorting essential societal functions, terrorist networking, skimming and credit card fraud, exposure of individuals (nude or embarrassing photos), deliberate disinformation, racism. The controversial 'surgical bombing' within the military field is always successfully performed by OUR side, while the enemy is shelling our women and children like crazy."

Do you have any additional comments, reflections, and/or experiences to share with us?

"ICT and its hardware is a young technology with too many weaknesses, still we already rely upon it too much. If a stupid little modem worth 150 euros is dysfunctional, the TV, fixed telephone lines and computers in a whole family home is at a standstill. And they dream about driverless coordinated cars which can run through city traffic at a 2–3 meter distance between the vehicles, driver drunk or sleeping without breaking the law, because the car is in charge, within 15 years or so . . . I've got my doubts!"

5.6.2 Interview with a day care teacher

"I think it is so good to belong to my generation, since through my parents I have access to the generation that did not have TV, telephones etc. when they were children, as did my parents. I myself did not have a computer or mobile as a child or youngster. I was blessed with free play outdoors. I also want to continue to write post cards and letters with slow mail instead of using the Internet for everything, even if it is very convenient and good in many ways.

"On the other hand, my own children grew up with all these technical things; they just are available everywhere without children having to reflect about this development. The negative things are that children just sit too long with their iPads and computers and phones, which could be harmful in many ways. The technologies are so accessible. Building trust is also essential; to have control and be present for the security of the children. It is too easy to end up on the wrong page. Children can be cheated.

"What I experience very negatively is that children do not themselves find out things they can do if they do not have access to the computers. I try to stimulate my children's creativity by taking them away from, and limiting the time at, the screen and encouraging them to busy themselves with other things. After Christmas we saved up cardboard boxes in the childcare center to make small houses and play puppet-theatre.

"The advantages of the technologies are that children could learn quickly various things. There are good, pedagogical games and films. Fantastic to be able to find information quickly and easily, but with the presence of a grown-up.

"ICT is now introduced in preschools with small children, and the children are supposed to learn to use iPads in various ways. To take photos, use various effects such as light and sound, and take and look at pictures and film in a pleasant and creative way."

5.6.3 Letter from a female school physician

"I am for many years concerned about what kind of reality we are giving our children today. It is amazing how the young child's brain is developing in inter-action with the environment. What the child actually DOES has a fundamental importance for development of the brain. I am referring to the extremely interesting theory of the mirror neuron, and results showing the importance for the development of empathy through interplay with people as well as motor training – both are fundamental as a stimulus for the brain[1]. The entry of visual screens into children's lives represents a huge change. We don't really know what the impact will be on the growing brain. Personally, I think that working towards a good balance between digital and real life is important – that adults must help children to limit their screen time so they don't miss too much of real life. Daily, I have patients who feel uncomfortable due to lifestyle issues where screen time often is extreme. Mental illness is increasing among young people in Sweden and school results are going down. I keep arguing that children are wonderful new-baked human beings who can get a fantastic life – with proper support from the grown-up world."

5.6.4 Interview with a young girl of 10 years

If you would drop your mobile phone and not be able to buy a new one until after one week, what would you miss the most?

"I would feel unsafe in case anything happens, the same kind of feeling when I happen to travel too far with the bus. I would not be able to know what come to pass with my friends on social media. I would feel as if I was living under a stone, would not be able to communicate with my friends on doing something." The three years younger sister also jumps into the room and adds: "To play, not be able to call".

You and your class mates are often using mobiles: iPhone or iPad. What do you like the most? What functions do you use most often?

"YouTube, Instagram, Snapchat and Musical.ly. Most frequently I check on YouTube-videos". The sister adds "I check the Children's Chanel on Swedish and Television Play, on iPad or the computer".

What do you like the least? What can make you sad/angry?

"One become sad when one look at the Snapchat and Mystery function and seeing that a close friend (kompis) is together with somebody else and writing "I am with my best friend (bästis)". Sister adds: "When WIFI does not work."

Is there anything that you would like to improve as to your and your friends' use of computers and mobile phones?

"That we were allowed to use the mobile phones during breaks at school. That the camera could give better photos – a bit more similar to reality".

Anything else you want to tell me?

"It would be good if we had a better WIFI at home, a quicker WIFI. It would be good if the batteries of the mobile lasted longer and that one could "give" battery time to ones friends."

Sister: "It would be good if those persons on SVT play did not show the same program again and again. And if one could have the mobile under the water".

5.7 Interviewing myself in 2013

Stimulated by the answers given by the survey respondents, back in 2013, I decided to interview myself, in order to understand what I personally thought about ICT and its effects on my own life over the years. I later contrast those 2013 answers to how I felt in 2016.

How did my life change?

Very much so, ICT became the main research field.

Most positive? Most positive is that I have devoted my life to an essential "causal factor", ICT, that most dramatically is changing the world and people's lives on all continents. In that respect, I have been able to feel meaningfulness in my work. The winds were blowing in all directions over the years, but I could take the hard winds by knowing that I brought to this field valuable experiences and perspectives. Now since I am formally retired, I still try to focus on how I best can contribute to an awareness of the societal and psychosocial effects of ICT – what is negative and positive about it for human beings.

In my private life, it is now easy to *coordinate family* meetings and all kinds of gatherings. Recent hardware facilitates a lot – I think of my iPad or iPhone, and that it is so *easy to enlarge the text*. My "Googling" mostly takes place on *the sofa*.

Most negative? I feel a kind of *new split, a divide*. Some new elements in my life *prohibit a full presence*. It is like a "shadow life" has entered. It is not only "here and now", but also a parallel reality that calls for you. It is around you all the time – in all mobile equipment. This divide did not exist during the pre-IT era. I am sometimes longing to meet again these pre-IT persons but most have now passed away. There seems to have been more time before, people were not stressed. At the same time I feel *enriched* by the access to and use of ICT and privileged to be able to reach out, to connect to human beings that I never would otherwise be able to interact with. I feel more of a *world citizen* and get a richer identity and deeper understanding of people independent of background – social, cultural, and religious. This is sometimes also tiring – the world is entering my pocket.

Most negative? Most negative is that people tend to value their presence in cyberspace, which often has a negative impact on the quality of the personal face-to-face relationships. In addition, unforeseen and unplanned personal meetings become rare.

What is quality of life (or a good life) for you?.

Quality of Life is one way to summarize the fulfillment of human needs. I reflect on quality of life in a structure of analytical levels which are mutual interdependent. Basically it is about Love in its various shapes, and originating from various sources/levels.

Three most important aspects that contributes to quality of life?

Good health physically and psychologically and also for people around me – that family and close friends do not go into irreversible health declines. It is important that:

- warmness and trust dominate around you
- society and community are functioning as an extended home as to shelter, food, security for all
- democracy works in all its dimensions and all areas of life
- the societal conditions in progress seem to become good for the coming generations. The feelings that our parents' generation had, were often a conviction that the next generation (their children) would have a better life than themselves. There are new threats now of quite a different kind.

What impact on the quality of life in society has ICT had in general?

Unemployment remains as a permanent problem and is a high risk in the Western culture.

In 1973 I initiated a research program at Stockholm University which I gave the title "Rationalization and Its Impact on Working Environment of Salaried Employees" (RAM). At that time, people were scared that computers would replace them at work and large-scale unemployment would occur. "Computer Anxiety" appeared as a name for this phenomenon. An agreement existed between the Swedish labor market and political parties that the computer was a tool to make industry more effective, so that it would be possible to shorten the working hours and continue with the welfare society and for manual workers to become free from heavy and dangerous work environment and for salaried employees to be rid of monotonous work.

The tools of effectiveness became smaller, cheaper, and more powerful and were "married" with telecom technology, media technology. They became ICT, and ICT later converged with VR as a new 'lady'.

Statistics show that Sweden has one of the most effective production industries in the world, and that Swedish working life is very effective in general. Further there has been *a move towards individualism and high consumption* and the psychosocial pressure is increasing according to figures about stress related diseases.

Unemployment for younger people is too big all over Europe. *A rethinking is needed* that deals with life style, values, and allocation of resources. Innovation of all kinds regarding welfare systems with regard to elderly people, school, health care. We could have a *dream society*. What are the strategies?

Permanent employment disappeared. In the present flexible working life there are fewer and fewer people in permanent jobs; *Flexibility* has its price – an insecure situation, it is hard to plan for private life and family. This new situation on the labor market needs some sort of "back-up" from society. More initiatives for creating meaningful work situations within areas that need labor. Both unemployed people and workers with short contracts have negative side effects on health.

How would you characterize the present era and people's lives with regard to society and technology?

Within Swedish society, there is a move *from collectivism to individualism*: in a first step, this is due to changes of political system and the broad and deep use of ICT. In a next step, there seems to have grown an *increase of activism* in certain areas*, a newborn collectivism*, supported by social media and the open source movement. There is a reaction against consumerism.

An increased speed and tempo in general. There is a *less caring for privacy* in parallel with openness. There is an increased willingness to share personal experiences.

Flexibility, stress insecurity, entertainment, and news are all mixed.

Strengthening of the Self through Google (knowledge) and through exercise (body). I am surprised that mobile technology and strong electronic networks did not break the present trend of urbanization and growth in mega cities.

> **Most important:** everybody can access "the world of knowledge" without cost – so far. Everyone can at least theoretically reach everyone else.
>
> **Most negative:** ICT seems to be an independent power, which cannot be stopped and redirected. It is deeply involved in globalization which is mutually interdependent on ICT. At a final stage, it is a balance of between the Good and the Evil powers in life. This is why ICT should first of all be used to develop the deeply humane part of people. Civic Intelligence and Civil Personal Growth have to go hand in hand.
>
> **Opportunities:** There are wonderful opportunities for peace and collaboration, deeper understanding, and narrowing the big splits between

cultural, economic, political, religious systems. Learn to develop a unity within diversity.

Risks: Cyber war. The "Big Data" problem. Awareness and Actions are needed.

Big existential issues tend to be drowned by the massive amount of information and communication circulating around, and to be manifested in detail in mobile apps.

5.8 My answers in 2016

In parallel with finalizing this little book, I have been invited either to talk or to be interviewed a few times, first at the inauguration of "Gunilla Bradley Research Center for Digital Business" at Linnaeus University in Växjö and Kalmar in Sweden, then interviewed for two journal articles (for Smålandsposten and the KTH Magazine), and have given a keynote address at the IADIS conference on "ICT Society and Human Beings" in Madeira in Spain in summer 2016.

Before such meetings or events, I write down the issues or points that I am eager to tell and that are based in my own and others' research. So what are my answers on that basis, and from my current notes and visuals? I feel that maybe the questions in the interview guide should be *modified* or *sharpened*. I will return to that in the final two chapters of this book. Also, during some days of writing on this book, one of my daughters asked me to take care of her family cat. This gave me some opportunity to reflect on the notion of speed/exertion and abeyance/repose.

What are my current concluding answers to questions that dealt with the more *general changes* connected to the use of ICT? What are the *good things* and what are the *bad things*? I will summarize these in Chapter 6 entitled "The Good ICT Society". From an impressionistic view about Life in the ICT Society in the second decade of the 21st century, I will proceed to the final chapter on "Actions to reach the Good ICT society" (Chapter 7).

Note

1 Iacoboni, M. (2009). Imitation, Empathy, and Mirror Neurons. *Annual Review of Psychology*. Vol. 60: 653–670.

6   The Good ICT Society

- What is a good quality of life? A vision
- From an information society for all to quality of life for all
- The humane element – humanization
- What is a Good ICT Society?
- Bibliography
- Appendix (Chapter 6)

6.1 What is a good quality of life? A vision

Dear Reader,

Let us revisit the interviewees and their voices just for a moment. People told us about what they thought are the most important things for having a good quality of life, answering the question, "What does quality of life (or 'a good life') mean for *you* and what contributes most to a good quality of life for you?"

Several people responded with the following very tangible and real world things or qualities. The bullet points below are from three individuals:

- Healthy food; well-constructed shelter; robust physical health; close, trusted and trusting friends; reliable, clean public transportation; reliable, reputable sources of news and information; structured educational materials (for use in teaching or self-improvement); an open, tolerant mind; patience; a range of useful, demanding, rewarding (to oneself and to others) activities; time to reflect.
- Sustainable environment, possibility for creative work for all, common ownership and control of the economy, participatory democracy, and an integrative culture that enables learning and social interaction of all.
- Feeling secure, having a home, loved ones, family, friends, not fearing to lose basic functions as a stable home, food, and amenities for you and your family. Living in a society that is equal, democratic, and open, where all are treated with respect and have good living conditions.

I also want to point out that others responded that different kinds of **freedom** are important: for example, being able to do what they want and when. Others mentioned **some specific issues** like having a job; earning enough; being healthy; receiving immediate health care or a doctor's help when needed; and having access to the Internet and phone. Having a **good work-life balance** was often mentioned. People value **psychosocial and philosophical aspects** as well, less tangible things such as continuously learning things and enjoying a proper balance and *enjoying all the senses* of our bodies. You might recall from the previous chapter that people long for engagement in worthwhile work, and maintain ideals such as equality and democracy, openness, and respect. They feel the need for a sense of community; an interesting job that provide *contributions to the community* and the environment; a lifestyle with a low environmental impact; good relationships with family and friends with whom one can talk and think about *"real" issues and trying to do something* about them. People value *peace and freedom, quietness and beauty* of nature, *happiness* and joy.

These tangibles and intangible issues all interact in different arenas: ecology, economy, politics, and culture. I think that, in general, the main aspect for having a good life and quality of life concern *very basic factors, and it is important to reflect on where technology has taken us and where we want to go from now.*

Getting to where we are now as researchers in ICT, has taken decades – and not just decades of technological developments. When finishing various projects and books over the years, I often wrapped them up by specifying some desirable goals and visions for the ICT society or computer society. Sometimes I formulated these as *research* for the future or *policy statements*. I was a technology researcher with a psychology background working among informatics people, and was sometimes fed up with the surrounding research and conferences on system development and new strategies for Information Systems (IS), and so forth.

I can trace my ways of thinking through time, as I have done in several previous chapters, starting in the 1970s and continuing until today. In the 1970s and 1980s, technology researchers examined the big leaps that were about to come in ICT: we worried about the data processing arms race, where technology was embraced without looking for its bad sides. The early use of display terminals replaced work at wooden desks; there was the arrival of personal computers (PCs) and distributed computer power; the use of PCs in homes; the micro computerization related to ever smaller, more powerful, and cheaper chips; the early use of applied artificial intelligence (AI) in the 1980s; the start of the mobile life and smart phone era. At each stage, our research pointed out both benefits and risks. Social research came to deal with people's whole personal lives, the economy, and more.

By the mid-1990s, as people embraced the thinking about these issues, the convergence of increased computer power with communication technologies, such as the Internet and personal handheld devices, meant that the proposed paradigm shifts were now reality. Here's what researchers in the 1990s predicted would happen (Ewerman, 1996):

Present world view	*Future world view*
Political ideology	Individual ideology
Global	Local
Large-scale	Small-scale and large-scale
Professionalism	Amateurism
Knowledge	Knowing
Taking apart	Bringing together
Mastering nature	Nature as a source for inspiration

My vision as it stands today has evolved over the past several decades, formed from a mix of my theoretical perspective in progress which still continues to develop even today, empirical work, and some insights from my background as both a behavioral scientist and a psychologist. I focused mostly on the middle of the convergence model, "Effects on Human Beings" (see Chapter 3). But when presenting action strategies for the good ICT society, I used a picture of a *Tree of Action* that addressed changes on all levels of analysis and that corresponded to all the clusters of circles in the current convergence model. You will read more about the Tree of Action in the final chapter of this book. But, before those actions can be taken, I will present to you my conception of the Good ICT Society.

6.2 From an information society for all to quality of life for all

Over the past two decades, I have proposed that the following seven challenges need to be considered in order to arrive at a Good ICT Society. In particular, I explore the aspects of humanization in more detail in section 6.3 of this chapter.

- *Integration*: ICT should contribute to enrichment in the social contact between people and should be used to prevent social isolation and facilitate integration.
- *Autonomy*: ICT should contribute to greater autonomy for the individual. Control or freedom is a classic issue often described in terms of 'privacy – integrity'.
- *Balance/harmony*: ICT should facilitate information access for all and support individual learning, but at the same time prohibit various kinds of overload, e.g., information overload, contact overload.

- *Humanization*: ICT should contribute to the deepening and development of true human qualities and be used to provide time for people to develop themselves as human beings.
- *E-cooperation (peace)*: e-conflicts must be avoided. E-cooperation and peace are major concerns.
- *Synthetic thinking and acting*: There is a need to focus on *syntheses*.
- *Human welfare* and *life quality for all*: Research to achieve these two aspirations, which are the crucial societal goals.

Balance between the rational and emotional parts of life – between the traditional male and traditional female aspects was a goal pointed out in my early writings in the 1970s.

As the 21st century turned, I emphasized *psychosocial and structural processes* to reach goals such as:

- *Information access* for all
- *Well-being and quality of life* for all
- *Enrichment* in the social contact between people
- *Integration* and respect for *diversity*
- Greater *autonomy* for the individual
- Prevention of various kinds of overload and stress
- Deepening of true *human qualities*
- Deepening and broadening of *democracy*
- E-cooperation and *peace*
- *Sustainability* in a broad sense, including the environment, economy, and the human side of life

Today, I would add that *preparing for the unforeseen* – for natural and human-made catastrophes – has become of utmost importance as a technique or process.

As we entered the new millennium, I also added *globalization* to this list of concerns: How does the strong interaction between globalization and ICT affect culture, economy, and labor? At the beginning of digitalization the digital divides and gaps were heightened by ICT, but that gap seems to even out. However, ICT has become a weapon and is now a threat for the survival of present-day societal structures. This is a sneaking and invisible process. I would say that we have entered the era of *e-war and digital war*. Highly professional programmers have built new types of virus attacks with and/or without informed governments. The targets have included societal structures (from the digital giants/companies such as Microsoft to many email and web servers). Organized criminal actions and e-sabotage highlight the *vulnerability* – and insecurity – of society as well as the dependency we have as people on ICT. This has resulted in huge challenges concerning TRUST in the many aspects of our ICT lives. ICT is related to both peace and war (see Chapter 4).

At the same time, ICT obviously has the *potential for promoting health and well-being*. ICT is a beautiful technology – *with a high potential for helping humans create a good society for all – an embryo for democracy, well-being, health, quality of life for all*.

At the first World Information Technology Forum (WITFOR) in 2003, conference participants created the first *official statement* in the direction of my visions. The following major goals were stated at the meeting (see also Chapter 1):

*   *bridging the digital divide* between rich and poor in the world; urban and rural societies; men and women; and different generations;
*   ensuring the *freedom of expression* enshrined in Article 19 of the Universal Declaration of Human Rights;
*   *reducing poverty* through the use of education and ICT;
*   *facilitating the social integration* of excluded segments of societies;
*   respecting linguistic and cultural *diversity*;
*   fostering the creation of public domains with full respect of *intellectual property rights*;
*   supporting communities in *fighting illiteracy*;
*   encouraging *e-governance and e-democracy* initiatives;
*   improving the *quality of life* through effective *health service systems*;
*   protecting the local and global environment for *future generations*.

6.3 The humane element – humanization

My vision for the ICT society concerns the humanization of life conditions. One way to formulate this is to use the *Declaration of Human Rights*. But what is "human"? This question is being discussed with the recent development and *use of human-like robots* and involves many ethical challenges.

The list below, with some short comments on each of the key words, originates from Schultz (1994). The phrasing "human element" is applicable primarily in democratic societies but is thought-provoking and gives strengths to human beings.

*   *dimensions*: inclusion, control, and openness are basic dimensions of human functioning;
*   *self-esteem*: the core of each person, from which one derives creativity, motivation, and productive work issue: all behavior derives from self-esteem;
*   *truth*: the grand simplifier, energizer, and clarifier;
*   *choice*: we choose our own life – thoughts, feelings, memories;
*   *simplicity*: often the most profound solution;
*   *holism*: all aspects of a person (thoughts, behavior, feelings, body) are interrelated;

- *completion*: joy and effectiveness are enhanced by the completion of unfinished experiences;
- *collaboration*: poor collaboration does not arise from differences but from rigidities, which result in low self-esteem;
- *empowerment*: only through giving power;
- *accountability*: everyone involved is 100 per cent responsible;
- *ethics*: if people feel good about themselves, they act ethically.

I now have the hindsight to reflect on several of the WITFOR and WSIS conferences, in the early part of the 21st century, that I was privileged to attend. I am also able to compare their content and statements to how all these ideas have developed more recently in 2013–2016. I am also in a position to compare the visions set out in these international conferences with my own concepts and what I call visions.

The 2003 WITFOR meeting was followed up by the *World Summit of Information Society* (WSIS), which is mainly held in developing countries; at this conference, NGOs and civic society also get involved. (Indeed, the last one in the series in autumn 2016 was held in Costa Rica.) The WITFOR and WSIS events can be seen as an important *awareness process* of the potentials connected to ICT. At the WSIS meetings in Geneva in 2003 and in Tunis, 2005, a wide range of players worked together to develop principles and prioritize actions to move towards democratic, inclusive, participatory, and development-oriented information societies at the local, national, and international levels. Issues addressed during the Tunis WSIS 2005 meeting included social justice, human rights, internet, and global governance, and more.

The 2003 summit was expected to identify and articulate new development possibilities and paradigms, possible in the information society, and to develop public policy for realizing these opportunities *to achieve social justice, financing, and people-centered actions*. At an early stage, the conference participants agreed that our future information society must be based on the Universal Declaration of Human Rights – including civil and political rights, as well as social, economic, and cultural rights. To move from declarations and commitments into actions seems to be the big challenge.

Internet governance and global governance are necessary in a world that is increasingly more connected and interdependent. The role of the United Nations system as the present legitimate inter-governmental forum becomes, ever increasingly, a key question. If I were attending the summit today, I would also raise issues of *global surveillance*.

In Tunis in 2005, improvements in civic society *participation* in the WSIS processes were achieved, and roles and responsibilities for civil society were specified.

Issues that the civil society addressed in Geneva and Tunis at the WSIS meetings are listed below with some comments on two of the issues. Some issues have come to the fore over the past decade. "Children" and "ethics", for example, which were of big concern in 2013.

- *Gender equality*
- *Culture, knowledge, and the public domain*
- *Education, research, and practice*
- *Media*: Freedom of expression
- *Health information*
- *Children and young people in the information society*: Strategies are needed to protect children and young people from the risks from new technologies, including access to inappropriate content, unwanted contact and commercial pressures (pornography, pedophilia, and sexual trafficking) while at the same time respecting freedom of expression. *The views of young people* are needed in shaping the new ICT world.
- *Ethical dimensions*: Ethical values brought up at WSIS were respect for peace and the fundamental values of *freedom, equality, solidarity, tolerance, shared responsibility, and respect for nature, trust, stewardship and shared responsibility, digital solidarity, and social cohesion.*

The WSIS Forum 2013 focused on the future of ICT, particularly as an engine of growth in a post-2015 development environment. Participants engaged in discussions on a number of diverse topics, such as ICT infrastructure, cyber security, enabling environment, e-learning, e-health, e-agriculture, media, accessibility, and ethics. High-level dialogues with government ministers and representatives from business and civil society examined:

- Women's empowerment in the Information Society: systematic, scalable strategies
- Smart climate change monitoring: Expanding access to information on weather, climate, and water
- ICT innovations and standards
- Securing cyberspace in a borderless world
- Youth and ICT

I think that the so-called Arab Spring in 2011 and other similar movements that followed many of these early conferences can be viewed as good examples of the power of ICT – for change and for hope. There is much human suffering but also learning and progress related to these events, which hopefully in the next steps would facilitate strivings for "a better world". At a time of writing this book I perceive, nevertheless, a deep backlash in the world regarding the promising efforts to use ICT in striving towards democracy.

The most recent WSIS Forum 2016 addressed many similar issues which have evolved in different ways. They include women's rights online; telecommunications infrastructure; spam; rights of persons with disabilities; privacy and data protection; other human rights; online education; multilingualism; freedom of expression; e-money and virtual currencies; e-commerce; domain name system (DNS); digital divide; development; cybersecurity; cybercrime; cultural diversity; content policy; child safety online; capacity development; access; and actors.

6.4 What is a Good ICT Society?

Today, I would say that my reflections and thinking on "the Good ICT Society" must be joined to those of the "The Sustainable Society": the UN agreed 17 Sustainable Development Goals for Agenda 2030 (see Appendix 1, Chapter 6).

Now we have a set of guidelines that could help the world to unify and would serve as political goals for all nation states of the world. We all have the same goal in common – and that is to survive and act in order to provide the next generations with the best prerequisites to survive and have "a good life".

The *Sustainable Development Goals* have action-oriented formulations and address many of the concerns that are valid for the Good ICT Society – some of them are about challenges that must be overcome, such as poverty, hunger, and inequality within and among countries, whereas others are about aspirations to strive for: well-being, equitable quality education and lifelong learning opportunities for all, gender equality, sustainable management of water and sanitation for all, modern energy for all, economic growth and employment for all, sustainable industrialization and innovation, human settlements, sustainable consumption and production patterns, actions to combat climate change, sustainable use of the oceans, seas and marine resources, sustainable use of terrestrial ecosystems, access to justice, and global partnership for sustainable development.

A Good ICT Society should strive to assist in meeting those goals. There is a logic in looking back at various rules and laws developed in the past.

At this stage in development, there is reason to remind us of the **Three Laws of Robotics.** These were a set of rules devised by the science fiction author and Boston professor Isaac Asimov and introduced in his short story "Runaround" in 1942:

1   A robot may not injure a human being or, through inaction, allow a human being to come to harm.
2   A robot must obey the orders given it by human beings except where such orders would conflict with the First Law.

3   A robot must protect its own existence as long as such protection does not conflict with the First or Second Laws.

Many of Asimov's stories involve robots behaving in unusual ways as an unintended consequence related to the three laws. In his later fiction where robots had taken "responsibility" for government of whole planets and human civilizations, Asimov added a fourth law: A robot may not harm humanity, or, by inaction, allow humanity to come to harm. The laws are referred to in many books, films, and other media.

In the tradition of Asimov's focus on the importance of rules and laws, I would like to mention three possible principles relating to ICT:

ICT must be beneficial for humans and nature.
ICT must serve all and be available for all.
ICT must promote the "golden rule".

Reflecting on past developments and historical research, it becomes evident that the questions raised in my own research during the first period of computerization are still relevant today: What type of society do we wish to have in the future? What life conditions do we want? What factors are contributing to well-being, creativity, and trust in the future? As we have moved from ICT use in a limited way to an ICT society that exists on a global scale, these issues have widened. At the present technology stage, this set of questions could be extended to encompass:

* How can ICT be used for *dialogue* in the world?
* How can research improve that dialogue? How can ICT and, more specifically, the Internet, SMSs, blogs, and Skype be used to promote dialogue between cultures, increase mutual understanding, and enrich us all?
* How can ICT be used to *prevent violence* and aggression using weapons? Violence creates violence. Instead, *worldwide dialogue and web-based non-violent actions in civil society* and at the grass-roots level can act as a new force in global politics.
* How can *human rights* be more deeply understood, exemplified, and applied in the ICT society? Who are the present players, and what new players globally are crucial to the promotion of *human rights in the ICT society*?
* How can ICT be used to *deepen human qualities and societal qualities*?

Visions and actions can be formulated in various ways and with different focuses and perspectives. However, to get closer to the individual again, physical and *psychosocial environment, human needs, human requirements, and human rights must be brought to the fore.*

We can all be *actors* in this process. We all have a responsibility – politicians, NGOs, companies, researchers, IT professionals, customers and, not least, the *individual* – to get involved. In the current era, there is a need for *unified actions* and IT strategies to support the *survival of future generations* as well as assuring a healthy psychosocial life environment for present and coming generations. A tree of action can symbolize the efforts to reach these goals. We are in a unique position in history, one where we should take on the responsible to use the technology to promote peace and deepen democracy and the quality of life for all.

This was the main reason why Diane Whitehouse and I organized a series of panels internationally in Italy, Sweden, Portugal, and Denmark during the period 2011–2013. These events provided many rich and multifaceted insights and experiences on how to move all the formal statements and agreements internationally practically into the daily lives of each and every one of us – as individuals, family members, workers, citizens, and inhabitants of the globe.

Ultimately, my long walk over the past two decades has been from "Visions on the Good Society" to "The Good ICT Society" to "The Good ICT Society for All" to "The Sustainable Society for the Planet".

Bibliography

Asimov, I. (1942). *Runaround.* Astounding Science Fiction, March, 1942.

Asimov, I. The Robot Novels: *I, Robot,* (1950) ISBN 0-553-29438-5; *The Rest of the Robots,* (1964) ISBN 0-385-09041-2; *Robot Dreams,* (1986) ISBN 0-441-73154-6.

Bradley, G. (ed.) (2008). Book of Proceedings of the IADIS International Conference: ICT Society and Human Beings, within MCCSIS (Multi-Conference on Computer Science and Information Systems). Amsterdam, The Netherlands, July 22–24, 2008. IADIS Press.

Bradley, G., Whitehouse, D., Singh, G. (eds.) (2011). Book of Proceedings of the IADIS International Conferences: ICT, Society and Human Beings, and eDemocracy, Equity and Social Justice, within MCCSIS. Rome, Italy, July 20–26, 2011. IADIS Press.

Bradley, G., Whitehouse, D., and Lin (eds.) (2012). Book of Proceedings of the IADIS International Conferences: ICT, Society and Human Beings, and eCommerce, within MCCSIS. Lisbon, Portugal, July 17–23, 2012. IADIS Press.

Ewerman, A. (1996). *Marknaden 1000 År – Fem eror i Europa (The Market 1000 Years – Five Eras in Europe).* Stockholm: Ewerman Business Intelligence AB.

Schultz, W. (1994). *The Human Element.* San Francisco: Jossey-Bass Publishers.

The Sustainable Development Goals (SDGs), Officially Known as Transforming Our World: The 2030 Agenda for Sustainable Development. www.un.org/sustainable development/sustainable-development-goals/

Universal Declaration of Human Rights – the United Nations. www.un.org/en/udhrbook/pdf/udhr_booklet_en_web.pdf

Appendix 1 (Chapter 6)

Sustainable development goals

- Goal 1. End poverty in all its forms everywhere
- Goal 2. End hunger, achieve food security and improved nutrition, and promote sustainable agriculture
- Goal 3. Ensure healthy lives and promote well-being for all at all ages
- Goal 4. Ensure inclusive and equitable quality education and promote lifelong learning opportunities for all
- Goal 5. Achieve gender equality and empower all women and girls
- Goal 6. Ensure availability and sustainable management of water and sanitation for all
- Goal 7. Ensure access to affordable, reliable, sustainable, and modern energy for all
- Goal 8. Promote sustained, inclusive and sustainable economic growth, full and productive employment and decent work for all
- Goal 9. Build resilient infrastructure, promote inclusive and sustainable industrialization, and foster innovation
- Goal 10. Reduce inequality within and among countries
- Goal 11. Make cities and human settlements inclusive, safe, resilient, and sustainable
- Goal 12. Ensure sustainable consumption and production patterns
- Goal 13. Take urgent action to combat climate change and its impacts*
- Goal 14. Conserve and sustainably use the oceans, seas, and marine resources for sustainable development
- Goal 15. Protect, restore, and promote sustainable use of terrestrial ecosystems, sustainably manage forests, combat desertification, and halt and reverse land degradation and halt biodiversity loss
- Goal 16. Promote peaceful and inclusive societies for sustainable development, provide access to justice for all and build effective, accountable and inclusive institutions at all levels
- Goal 17. Strengthen the means of implementation and revitalize the global partnership for sustainable development.

7 Tree of Action

ICT is a field of research that is complex and changing, at accelerated speeds. We need much stronger support internationally for cross-disciplinary, cross-cultural, and action-oriented research on the topic of "ICT for Deepening of Humane and Societal Qualities".

With distributed computer power, strong telecommunications (e.g., the Internet) and mobile equipment, we have an inherent opportunity for deepening democracy and strengthening the skills of individuals and their influence on society. However, there is also an increasing risk that we end up enforcing centralization and misusing power. Achieving the *visions and goals* for the Good ICT Society for human beings (see Chapter 6) deserves stronger recognition as well as *action strategies* on all levels of society – including the global level.

In the last chapter of this book, I will lay out the actions I see as necessary to achieve a Good ICT Society. First, however, I'd like to lay out some of the thinking behind my road map, and the end point and purpose of this book. It means that I will go through the steps that it took me to formulate some principles and actions that I eventually call my own manifesto. I will present these main steps in section 7.1–7.4. They show how I have been influenced by the formulation of a tree of actions, and what that means at various societal levels and to others, to then explore the meaning of manifestos and how my own work can be understood as such a manifesto. Sections 7.5 and

7.6 then lay out what can be considered as the top 10 principles to facilitate a Good ICT Society, and the top 10 actions that can help achieve it.

For those readers who do not want to read that background, please go straight to section 7.7, "Summary of the Good ICT Society – from theory to actions".

7.1 Trees of action

Much of my work has been built on a Tree of Action. These trees have changed over the years. There is every reason to look back at several of them, including, for example, the individual level and the corporate or organizational level. However, do we need structures and levels for societal change in the network era at all? What was behind the levels in my original tree of action – that emerged well before the Internet and web?

Let me present what can be behind these levels, and what tools and strategies are connected to these levels. Figure 7.1 was derived during the first phases of computerization and reflects the way the introduction of technology was handled in a country like Sweden with the so-called Swedish Model. Particularly in its national and company-related branches, it focuses on matters relating to the welfare state, employers, and trade unions.

For such a tree of action to be valid in the 2000s, it has to be recognized that several changes have taken place as the implementation and use of ICT as well as in how organizations and companies operate. Examples are:

- One branch entitled '*the international level*' has come into play and a sub-branch for revitalization and revision of human rights should be added.
- One branch entitled '*the regional level*' has to be added.
- The branch entitled '*technology*' has to be divided into *three main sub-branches*: tele-technology, computer technology, and media technology due to increased capacity in each of these and due to the integration and convergence of these technologies. Sub-branches, such as nano-technology and biotechnology, have to be added.
- Regarding the '*organizational level*' branch, many factors have lost their steering functions in the new flexible companies, which are more often organized in networks as a result of the ongoing changes in work life. This is also the case for the public sector and civil society organizations.

Trade unions at the national level are not active in the same way as earlier, either in Sweden or in many other countries, in the fields of technology and the work environment, but have to adopt new strategies and collaborative

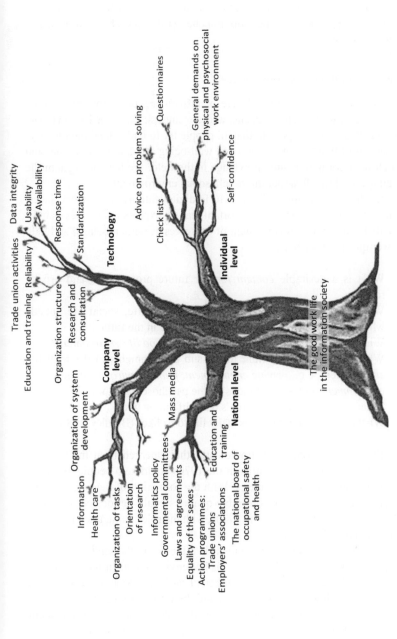

Figure 7.1 Tree of Action for computerization – before the Internet and web
Source: (Bradley, 1989)

structures. International collaboration between trade unions must be strengthened to balance the tension between capital and labor.

To sum up, new branches now grow out of the tree, and new sub-branches are appearing. Some branches/sub branches in the tree of action have lost their relevance.

The individual level: its importance

If people are to have a real chance of influencing their life situation, as workers, private persons, citizens, and consumers, they need knowledge. For that reason it is important that all people try to understand the underlying causes of both dissatisfaction and well-being at work and at home, and search for information and knowledge in the field. We have to reclaim the language used to talk about the psychosocial environment.

With the introduction and use of ICT (digitalization) in our workplaces, homes, and communities, it is important that we express our wishes as individuals for the future development of ourselves as human beings, and help answer questions such as:

- What is a desirable *content f*or our future professional and private roles?
- What *conditions of life* (leisure time, family life, social life outside what we now call work) do we wish to have in the future?
- What are the desirable characteristics of a *good life environment*?
- What qualities do we want in the sub environments of the total life environment, e.g., *private environment, public environment,* and *work environment* with special focus on the psychosocial aspects?
- What do we want our children's daily life to be like?
- What do we want our parents' daily life to be like? (Bradley, 1986, 1989)

The theories and conceptual frameworks that emerged from the Swedish model/Nordic work life research in the 1970s could help people to formulate and reflect on these qualities. With the formation of *new digital roles* in private and public areas, desirable qualities could be located in various roles – not solely as it was in the 1970s, with the roles being associated with professional and work lives.

On a personal level, the individual is affected by the environment, but the person also has an effect upon his/her environment. In most democracies people have been given a number of tools at national and corporate levels, such as laws and agreements, and the conditions have been created for broad-based action to improve the work environment and work content, and bring about change in the corporate as well as the societal environment. More people are also becoming their own bosses as freelancers and as entrepreneurs. But it is up to us as individuals to give our life its content, both in terms of desirable goals and the ways in which we can work towards attaining these goals. Thus this interplay is also an important factor when we take action in the field of new technology in general and new applications of ICT. Laws and agreements that support the individual in the work environment have, however, become weaker in the 2000s, at the same time that technology is reaching a stage that could strengthen the individual. Actions are needed to revitalize people's influence on their own lives.

The level of the individual is important – all organizations are made up of individuals. Phenomena at the corporate and collective level often reflect experiences or events at the national level and become part of our 'selves'. When we work to bring about change, for example, and when workplaces as well as homes are deeply penetrated by ICT, it is important that we feel 'good', i.e., that the scope for psychological defence mechanisms is minimized, and that we feel free and flexible. The work of bringing about change may sometimes have to be preceded by psychological or training courses that help people improve their self-confidence, so that we dare to voice our opinions and apply our experiences in co-creating a good psychosocial environment, which – in a next step – help individuals to grow as human beings.

The organizational and corporate level – psychosocial work environment: requirements and preferences

A set of classic questions that were raised early on in the field of computerization was which tasks are good for humans, which tasks are good for computers, and which tasks do human beings want to keep. This issue comes to the fore when more and more tasks and roles/functions are allotted to machines – mostly robots. We need a public discussion to anchor the next stages in ICT use. What important limits can we agree on? In which functions in society do we not want to introduce ICT?

History shows that when a technology is established, people tend to adapt to it, and the alternatives are erased. The human costs are hard to measure since, after a while, controlled studies between users and non-users of certain technologies or ICT applications cannot be undertaken. The already smaller, cheaper, more powerful technologies are *invisible and embedded* – the impact on humans can hence be described as an invisible and silent process, until a certain peak is reached. At the more and more advanced technological level in society, human beings and the civil society have to be involved, since the process is irreversible and concern ethical questions.

General psychosocial work environment requirements may be set out and put forward in many ways. How does this move operate with regard to the person's total life? The convergence of our life spheres and physical and psychosocial environments calls for a holistic perspective. It is of value to reflect on these aspects regarding life as a whole. Some aspects in our environment have been improved and facilitated – other aspects have been neglected.

Here some desirable working conditions are listed:

- A life pace that can be adjusted to suit individual capabilities (*workload per time unit*).
- A *reasonably even pace*, not too dependent on other people's pace and/ or equipment Too much pressure from market forces has negative consequences for individual and society.
- The opportunity to *influence* the structure and planning of work and working hours, e.g., the scheduling of breaks, the length of time at the screen, time when you are expected to be available outside of the formal working hours.
- The opportunity for *education (further education)* and *personal development.*
- The opportunity to satisfy *people's need for personal contact and communication in RL* as part of their daily life.
- An *adequate flow of information* so that the information reaches the people for whom it is intended.
- *Special support* to people whose life unavoidably involves them in the *intermediate position/buffer role (e.g., social workers)* and the negative effects of this position must be counteracted or prevented.
- Avoidance and prevention of physical strain on the *eyes, neck, and back muscles*; balancing moving and sitting still.
- A more even allocation of tasks between the sexes – so-called *extrinsic* equality.
- New professional roles and changes in jobs and positions that make use of the traditional male and female experiences, interests and values, i.e., so-called *intrinsic* equality.
- Professional roles that avoid the extremes of *overstimulation and understimulation*, which are both related to stress.

Human roles: a kind of meso level

The concept of role and role formation is common in social psychology. The two concepts refer to the various tasks, functions, and positions that an individual has in a certain context, including the norms and expectations associated with his or her position or tasks. In a flexible working life as well as in total life, we have to create our own roles and some *wisdom* needs to be applied. What is a proper available technology: hardware, software, and netware? What facilitates our work and what makes us happier? Sometimes we have to resist and say no to certain changes and rethink our priorities. When changes are taking place more broadly in workplaces – we have to work together collectively to express desirable changes in our roles. A distributed working environment requires a rethinking of proper meeting places as to time and space. Dependency, and sometimes addictiveness on the technology, can affect our roles and become health risks: the virtual part of the job content tends to increase. Most of us are becoming in some sense *digital workers*.

The challenges currently facing human beings in the ICT Society are enormous. Policymakers and politicians are often unable to handle such momentous decisions on their own. Citizens are therefore becoming increasingly involved in many realms of decision-making that are ICT-related. In this part of the chapter, I recount a number of experiences held throughout the last six or so years that have involved, on the one hand, senior academics, and on the other hand, young researchers, and have focused on a concern and consideration for the Good ICT Society and its involvement of young children.

My colleagues and I have held numerous panel sessions at various conferences, attempting to hammer out the optimal goals for the ICT Society (addressed in Chapter 6), and searching for ways to get to the Good ICT Society. We discussed different levels of change: societal, national, local, institutional, and organizational. We debated directions in values, lifestyles, individual cognition, and behavioural modifications. We also covered some national/governmental actions and international levels and actions as well as others that are feasible at both the individual level and the community level, whether physical or virtual.

An acceptance and introduction of *stakeholder approaches* are becoming more common, and are now included in planned international and national action programmes. For example, the European citizens' initiative was established as an EU legislative framework to discuss these issues (http:// ec.europa.eu/citizens-initiative/public/welcome). Different components of civil society will be more and more involved in taking these kinds of citizens' actions than ever before. *Citizens* are currently being encouraged to contribute positively to social change in their communities, and in the design and re-design of societal initiatives, as well as their supporting technologies. There is, of course, also the possibility that not all members of society will be interested in taking actions of any kind.

What has emerged from these many conference panel discussions are mind maps and an ever-evolving "tree of action(s)". One such mind map (see Figure 7.2) was developed at a panel discussion session held at the IADIS "ICT, Society, and Human Beings" conference in 2012 in Lisbon, Portugal. The discussion involved a tree of actions related to the developing world, research, and social capital and social production.

This kind of mind map helps to facilitate and stimulate creativity and encourage the sharing of "*civic intelligence*" among people who have quite different approaches to this broad field of computerization, and different

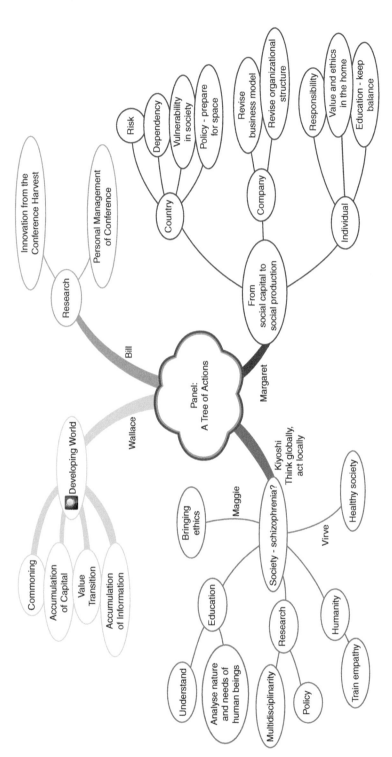

Figure 7.2 Mind map from a panel discussion on a Tree of Actions

kinds of foresight into the future of the ICT society. The important elements of this discussion lie in having *a shared conversation* that enhances growth in collaborative communication that takes place about the kind of world in which we want to live together in the future.

At the international conference ETHICOMP 2013, which was held in Kolding, Denmark, a panel of international experts offered their insights into possible future directions towards a Good Information and Communication Society. Hailing from different parts of the globe – the European Union, North America, Asia, and elsewhere – they explored what could be the beginnings of more definitive actions to reach that form of society. *We embarked on building a "tree of action" and a pattern of "interacting networks", acknowledging that we need both strategies.* As a metaphor for current and future action strategies, as well as for an illustration of the theoretical connections between the ideas, the *convergence model* was included in the trunk of the *Flower Tree of Actions* (see Figure 7.3).

The various actions, color-coded according to level, represent *a support system for decisions – we can all communicate with people at these different levels.* The panel discussion, which also included the audience members, expressed concern about both "the planet" and "quality of life" for people.

In this ETHICOMP panel, the panelists were asked in advance to reflect on the following questions: Could an international Code of Ethics or a Code of

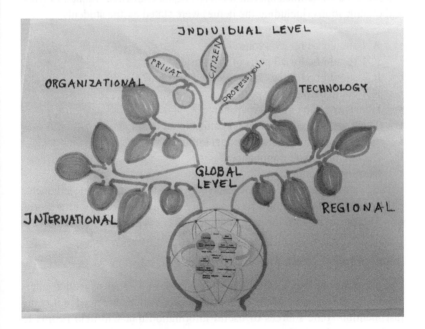

Figure 7.3 Flower Tree of Actions

Conduct for Citizens (the end users of ICT) be possible? Is a global approach feasible? What can we learn from the field of work of computer professionals? What should citizens be preparing themselves to do that will require more responsibility or accountability from themselves? How can we prevent a collective schizophrenia and promote empathy? What are the main challenges related to speed and acceleration of technology? What more effective solutions lie in the realm of Slow Tech (Patrignani & Whitehouse, 2014)? How can people benefit from, and master, the speed capacity of the technology instead of becoming slaves to the current paradigm of speed? Can grassroots movements take the lead towards a world free from cyber-attacks and the ICT armaments race? What is the role of different organizations in this field?

In a similar panel, held on "Building a tree of actions", organized at Linnaeus University, in April 2013, with doctoral and master students, a further discussion took place about some of the challenges at hand. While actions need to focus on individuals – for example, really vulnerable people in developing countries or emerging economies – they should also deal with the major societal challenges of the 21st century. The ideas discussed swirled around prevention and being more specific. It is no longer enough to generalize. Many of the answers exist in a much more networked environment and form of society. But still, actions and answers to these issues need to be balanced; the real quandaries we as human beings face will have complex and sometimes unclear answers. Some challenges related to work and organizations (including the home) were stated by the students:

- ICT should be for everyone
- ICT should be for all parts of the world
- ICT should be for the "bottom of the pyramid" (BOP)
- ICT could help elderly persons
- Homes could be more experimental
- Think about innovation and organizational learning
- Think about "materiality" and its implications
- Beware of market dominance
- Beware of monopolies
- Beware of the "superiority of academics" who try to make value judgments
- Analysis should not just be about "my" (individual) view of the world
- Values can be seen through many lenses

About children: screen time and gaming

The use of technology by children is a hot topic in Sweden as well as internationally; it is an area where both analysis and actions are needed. Let me just mention some sources of useful information that will help people to think about these challenges more in-depth.

According to the American Academy of Pediatrics, studies have shown that excessive media use can lead to negative impacts such as attention problems, school difficulties, sleep and eating disorders, and obesity (Strassburger et al., 2010).

The positive impact of playing computer games is primarily on the cognitive part of intelligence, e.g., language learning. Some games improve the spacial competence and work memory. Research priorities should be paid to children's roles in the ICT Society and be performed by transdisciplinary teams with, e.g., brain researchers, neuropsychologists, behavioral and social scientists. At the present stage of knowledge, it seems that a kind of precautionary principle should be applied and preventive actions are desirable. One example is a learning tool developed by Åse Victorin, a Swedish school and child physician (www.qleva.s/sv). The tool supports school children and their parents with how best to care about the brain, body, and each other, so as to have a good life in the ICT Society. On the basis of the medical studies which take account of the brain's psychomotoric development, we adults need to ensure that children and young people have a good balance between digital and real life (RL). Among the recommendations made are: Young children under 2 years should have no time on the screen other than short sessions spent together with parents; have happy screen-free days – it gives kids the freedom to do other things; have happy screen-free zones at home. These guidelines might be hard in cultures and countries where homes consist of a single room for all the family, but awareness creates automatically the possibility to find other strategies.

7.2 Different manifestos

I do not really like the word "manifesto" – it is an alien word, and it is not used in Swedish; it sounds "male" and somewhat central European. However, this book is a manifesto of sorts. There are, of course, other similar manifestos. For example, the Convivialist Manifesto was presented at a special session of the Summit Vienna meeting in 2015, which also introduced me to the *Onlife Manifesto*, a summary of the work of a group of European scholars that is followed by a set of short commentaries and essays (Floridi, 2015).

The *Onlife Manifesto* states that ICT is not only a tool, but it can also be seen as environmental constructs that affect self-conception (who we are); mutual interactions, conceptions of reality, and interactions with reality. Each of these elements has ethical, legal, and political significances.

Four major experiences are impacted by ICT:

* The blurring of the distinction between reality and virtuality
* The blurring of the distinction between human, machine, and nature
* The reversal from information scarcity to information abundance

- The shift from the primacy of stand-alone things, properties, and binary relations, to the primacy of interactions, processes, and networks

When reality changes too quickly, for example, due to ICT, our current conceptual framework does not work. There is then a risk that we make negative projections about the future. One goal of the *Onlife Manifesto* was to update our conceptual framework and avoid a philosophy of mistrust.

In 2014, a circle of 40 Francophone intellectuals agreed on the *Convivialist Manifesto* (See reference list) and it was soon published in an English translation at the Centre for Global Cooperation Research. This group of social scientists, who called themselves convivialists (from the Latin *convivere*, "living together"), speak warmly about a new art of cohabitation, based on a perceived urgency. Their criticism is mainly directed against the idea of "homo oeconomicus", which "economizes" the "social". The convivialists' alternative is based on the paradigm of "gift", formulated by the French sociologist Marcel Mauss, and further developed by Alain Caillé. The gift emphasizes reciprocity, trust, and mutual recognition, but at the same time accepts competing interests and conflicts.

Figure 7.4 Slow tech

A recent example of an ICT manifesto (or pre-manifesto according to the authors) that is much in line with my own approach can be found in the book *Slow Tech – Steps Towards a Good, Clean, and Fair Information and Communication Technology*, by Norberto Patrignani and Diane Whitehouse (2017). Part of these two authors' work is based on the fact that, in the 2010s, *time has become a psychosocial shortage.* This shortage has occurred despite the fact that we theoretically and practically have access to a technology that gives us more time than ever, a technology that can free us from paid work – both repetitive work and physically heavy work that dominated during industrialism and replaces more and more mental and cognitive work in the present net era.

Why did ICT not provide us with lots of free time to enjoy life, to increase the quality of life, and to care about nature? The authors point out a direction for how to develop a new roadmap that uses the keywords "Good, Clean and Fair", basing its origins in the principles that underpinned Slow Food. Good stands for human-centred, clean means environmentally sustainable, and fair shows a respect for human rights. The authors make an impressive analysis of the notion of slow, and point out directions to take to achieve desirable societal and human goals. The keywords "Good, Clean and Fair" serve as pearls in that chain.

Spending time looking after my daughter's family cat enabled me to experience my own form of Slow Tech in autumn 2016!

7.3 Towards an information society for all

When considering what it takes to move towards an information society for all, I would like to start at an international level, and then step back to Sweden, which I think has some interesting solutions to offer to other nations and to the global community.

Within the EU at the start of the 21st century, collaboration with regard to IT policy took place in the framework of the 'eEurope – An Information Society for All' initiative. In summary, the goals laid out were that, by 2005, Europe should have modern public services on the Internet; e-government; services for e-learning; e-healthcare services; and a dynamic environment for e-businesses. Technical requirements to facilitate the comprehensive access to broadband connections at competitive prices and a secure information infrastructure were specified. Responsibility for implementing eEurope 2005 was on the individual member states of the Union.

At the global level, collaboration concerning IT policy measures and positions took place within the framework of the World Summit on the Information Society (WSIS; see further Chapter 6 (6.3)). Today, what are the key issues with ICT and in the EU in 2017? Has the overwhelming migration of people from outside Europe to the continent become the main focus? Has ICT a new role to play? Are there ICT applications that could facilitate integration, primarily about giving information about the societal conditions in the emigrants' new country and learning the new languages? Educational applications could easily be translated to each of the current languages that are spoken by the migrants.

Swedish IT policy as an example on the national level

This section is built on many sources, mostly governmental documents. For detailed references I would recommend a Swedish doctoral thesis "Researching the Use of the Internet – A Beginner's Guide" (Selg, 2014).

In Sweden, there was an active "Computer Delegation" at the governmental level and several subcommittees of thoughtful computer scientists as early as the mid-1970s. The subcommittees dealt with a large number of areas. There were special committees on Employment; Work Environment; Security; Vulnerability in Society. The purpose, conclusions, and recommendations are still relevant and could be helpful to the present political work on what, again in Sweden, is called the digitalization process in society.

Much later, the so-called Swedish ICT Commission was set up. It was working around 2000 to contribute to the benefits of information technology in order to improve *quality of life for the population* and to increase the country's *international competitive standing*. With the proposal *An Information Society for All* (2000), the Swedish government set the objective for its IT policy – for Sweden to be *the first country to become an information society for all*. The action plan proposed actions within three prioritized areas:

* *Trust* in information technology
* *Competency* to use information technology
* *Access* to ICT; information society services made available to all

The specified goals and strategies were structured into working parties appointed by the Swedish government; an ICT strategy group; a Board for electronic government; a Democracy group; and a Forum for ICT and the environment.

Swedish ICT policy was then evaluated and *three demands* for IT policy were stated: A long-term perspective and a focus on strategic societal problem areas. Policy shall be consistent and enduring, that is, pedagogic. Policy shall be user-oriented and not product-oriented.

From "IT (ICT) policy for society" to "policy for the IT (ICT) society" was the expressive title of the Swedish government bill introduced in 2005, and the main goal was to be a sustainable IT society for all. The main goal was subdivided into three further sub-goals:

* IT should contribute to improving quality of life and to improving and simplifying everyday life for humans and companies
* IT should be used to contribute to sustainable growth

- An effective and secure IT infrastructure with a high level of transmission capacity should be available all over the country, for example, to provide human beings with interactive public e-services

The bill dealt with two necessary prerequisites for these three sub-goals to be achieved, which were specified as the importance of *trust* and the importance of *coordination*.

In *"ICT for Everyone – A Digital Agenda for Sweden* (Ministry of Enterprise, Energy and Communication, 2011), there was a special section on the role of ICT in societal development which emphasizes the following six important points:

- Digital information and digital tools should be used to a great extent in *research* activity and innovation processes
- ICT must contribute to an *environmentally* sound society
- *Gender equality* in the area of ICT is to be greatly improved
- In order to strengthen *freedom on the web*, Sweden must endeavor to ensure that human rights are respect on the Internet
- With the aim of *promoting creativity* and innovation it must be simple to council contract on copyright in the digital environment
- Use of ICT in development assistance must contribute to *poverty reduction, democratization, and respect for human rights.* Effective poverty reduction is promoted by openness in implement development assistance

The Swedish Digitalization Commission identified in late 2015 a number of strategic areas for future digitization policies: continuous state promotion, effective rules, and skills for the digital society, infrastructure, data-driven innovation, security, and privacy.

Most of the proposals laid down by the commission concern the labor market and the economy. Early intervention in schools and preschools are recommended to encourage girls to study technology, and there are proposals for financial incentives to individuals of the under-represented gender. Labor shortages in the IT sector are mentioned as one motivation to encourage women into the field. Another proposal is to develop a national strategy for data-driven innovation to solve the problems of global warming, energy shortages, and an aging population. The government should build up a national competence center around data-driven innovation. The Commission proposed a programme to upgrade skills for leaders in the Swedish municipalities to facilitate for them to contribute to welfare digitization. A further proposal is to establish a coordinating council for digital jobs. The purpose is to handle what is called the matching problem, where more and more job openings coincide at the same time with growing unemployment.

The Commission also proposed a general review of laws that obstruct the digitalization, and investigations of the "sharing economy" were initiated. The need to investigate the work environment in the digital economy due to distance work, flexible offices, and virtual organizations was also highlighted. Traditional physical mail handling should be phased out by the state authorities, and companies will have access to a digital mailbox for e-mails from the state. This would save money for the state, but will people still be able to choose to have traditional physical mail delivered to them?

In 2016, the Swedish Digitalization Commission has chosen to produce thematic reports about four areas of society that are being transformed by, but also transform, digitization. They are referred to as 1. The data-driven society, 2. Life-long learning in the digital society, 3. The social contract in a digital era, 4. Digitalization for sustainable climate. The purpose of the thematic reports is the educational, promotional, developmental, and policy driving aspects of digitalization. A public debate on all these matters is encouraged. The first report, "The Data Driven Society" 2016, deals with what questions the analysis of large amounts of data (big data) poses to our knowledge and understanding of human beings, society, and the environment, and what opportunities and challenges can be identified as a result.

In reviewing these steps, that have taken place at both the EU and Swedish level towards an information society for all, I ask myself: Where are the visions of a new and improved humane society? Maybe the answer is that ICT is now so completely a part of our lives and built into the societal fabric that, for now, we are merely fine-tuning the current socio-economic system until new unforeseen leaps occur. I find that unacceptable. Instead, acting now to discover what is truly human and what is truly desirable is crucial.

7.4 Where do we go from here?

Some more profound considerations and actions are needed at these fine-tunings of socio-economic conditions.

A *compass rose* is needed – one rose that all people could agree on regarding its *core direction.* I choose to insert again the rose from Chapter 4. One way forward would be to start to think in terms of the basic human needs – physical and psychosocial. For this reason, I refer back to the flower of human needs – see the chapter "In Search of Quality of Life and Wisdom in the ICT Society" (Chapter 2). We need to reconsider basic human *psychosocial needs and physical needs,* which I have illustrated throughout the years with a sunflower. Physical, basic needs are not met in all parts of the world. Poverty – insufficient access to food, water, and shelter – should not exist in the ICT Society.

Some developments, where consideration of human needs is fundamental in terms of the next industrial and commercial steps to be taken, include Robotics, Big Data, and Digital Business. The basic questions come up again: What work, services, and production do we as human beings want and what are we good at? What services do we want machines to do for us? What new *intermediaries* are important in the digital era?

Take a look again at the figures in Chapter 3 that illustrate the convergence model on ICT and Psychosocial Life Environment. How could actions towards a good and sustainable ICT Society be related to the convergence model and address humane sustainability? This challenge, and its answers, will be summarized in Figure 7.7. First, however, I will present what I would like to call my two manifestos in sections 7.5 and 7.6.

7.5 Manifesto – the top 10 principles for the Good ICT Society

On the development, introduction, and use of ICT, the main concerns are:

- *Democracy*: ICT should contribute to a deepening and broadening of democracy. Participation needs awareness and capacity building.
- *Human well-being* and *life quality for all* are the crucial societal goals, where both *psychosocial and structural processes* are needed.
- *Basic Human Needs*

    - Traditional physical needs concern shelter, food, and safety. Added to these should be body movement/exercise, human interaction in RL, training in humanity, and time spent in and near nature.
    - Basic psychosocial needs concern influence, learning and personal growth, social belonging, meaningful life content, and confidence.

- *Humanization*: ICT should contribute to the deepening and development of real human qualities such as empathy and capacity of cooperation, and be used to provide time for people to develop themselves as human beings.
- *Integration and respect for diversity*: ICT should contribute to enrichment in the social contact between people and should be used to prevent social isolation.

- *Autonomy*: ICT should contribute to greater autonomy for the individual. *Control* versus *freedom* is a classic tension often related to 'privacy – integrity'. ICT should ensure the *freedom of expression.*
- *Balance/harmony*: ICT should facilitate information and communication *access* for all and support individual *learning*, but at the same time prohibit various kinds of *stress*, e.g., information overload, communication overload, contact overload. A balance between spending time in virtual reality (VR) and RL is needed.
- *Sustainability*: ICT should contribute to sustainability in a broad sense, including the environment, economy, and human sustainability. Early information sharing in order to prevent any Internet bullying and abuse is needed. People around the world share the responsibility for the *next generations and the planet.*
- *Peace*: E-cooperation and peace are major goals.
- *Preparing for the Unforeseen*: Prepare for natural and human-made catastrophes. Vulnerability and insecurity should be replaced by *trust and transparency.*

7.6 Manifesto – the top 10 actions towards the Good and Sustainable ICT society

These 10 actions should be taken to achieve the Good and Sustainable ICT Society

- **World philosophy:** "The Golden Rule" should be the unifying kernel of a world philosophy that focuses on peace building.
- **Economic theories:** Economic theories should be revised in order to match the present ICT Society. Circular and sharing economies are to be developed. The huge challenges in the so-called digital economies have to be explored and analyzed.
- **Politics:** Should be built on common goals, for example, to address global warming, pandemics, and desirable livelihoods within the society. People need to actively care about human needs and keep up with natural rhythms that are universal. Universalizing and unifying also means caring about children's lives. More and more political realms become global and common – and have to bring nation states to collaborate.
- **International Agreements and Statements:** Human Rights, Agenda 2030, WITFOR, and WSIS are action tools, which all emphasize the need for increased knowledge, awareness, and respect for all people.
- **Education and learning:** "Preschool time" is fundamental for forming loving human beings and good global citizens. Topics, such as "Learning to be Humane and to Live in the ICT Society", "Stress Prevention", and "Critical Thinking" should be obligatory, from an early age.

- **ICT:** Guiding principles should include global disarmament to prevent cyber-attacks; open-source software; and digital commons. These offer examples of possible positive tools.
- **Labor market:** The content and the (re)design of new *professional roles* due to digitalization should give people meaning, influence, confidence, a sense of social belonging, and learning/personal growth. Components of future work life should be: full employment, shorter work hours, maximum/minimum salaries, work sharing, fair and ecological production, and globalization of trade unions to match the globalization of industry.
- **The allocation issue:** Computerization, IT, ICT, and digitalization are constantly creating a huge distribution problem, which is crucial to address for a Good ICT Society. At this accelerated change process actions should focus on:

  - **Distribution and balance:** Work and leisure; paid and unpaid work; production and reproduction; cities and rural areas.
  - **Distribution of resources and profit between:** Sectors within a country; countries and continents.

- **Empowerment:** Emancipation of both sexes should be facilitated. Empowering of women in both the private and public sector. Worldwide courses in emancipation for men at an early age should be developed.
- **Peace in the World:** Some examples of actions towards peace in the world, cited in detail in Chapter 4, are:

  - *Awareness* of the counterbalancing vulnerability of society needs to be built.
  - Use of cyberspace for *dialogue* and for the search for the common essence of all faiths, religions and philosophical and spiritual endeavors.
  - Exploration of strategies to *encourage humane roles* – emancipation is needed for men and women, as well as boys and girls.
  - Exploration of the power of *good examples* and the collaboration potential between formal and informal organizations *(networks) in peace building.*

To achieve peace in the world, one drastic action for the whole globe to agree on would be to convert the Global Weapons industry to an Eco and Renewable Energy industry – as result of the need to face the many unforeseen catastrophes, whether natural or human made.

Each of the 10 action points in this, my second, manifesto could have a dedicated book chapter of its own. Let me just, however, offer some more in-depth comments on 1 of the 10 points – education and learning. Living in an ICT Society adds to the notion of the "electricity society", in which there is still more independence and a "no limit life style". Limits outlined by both time and space disappear, and habits will develop that challenge humane sustainability. Schools are indeed places and environments where wisdom from the past and openness for new opportunities has to be balanced. There have been many words for this, like IT pedagogics, e-learning, and distance education. One book that handles actions in this field is *Teaching in the Digital Age* (Bates, 2015). The author addresses such questions as: How is the nature of knowledge changing, and how do different views on the nature of knowledge result in different approaches to teaching? What is the science and research that can best support teachers in their key societal role? How to maintain high quality in teaching in rapidly changing learning environments and, in parallel, manage the workload both for teachers themselves and students? What knowledge and skills are needed in a digital age, i.e., not mainly digital skills?

7.7 Summary of the Good ICT Society – from theory to actions

I would like to summarize this book with three graphical illustrations (Figures 7.5, 7.6, and 7.7) of a complicated new world in which engagement and actions from all of us are needed – keeping in mind the long-term and short-term goals and visions for the Good ICT Society. "Technology"

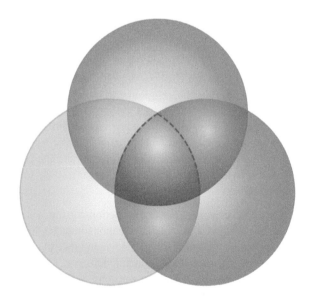

Figure 7.5 What is convergence?

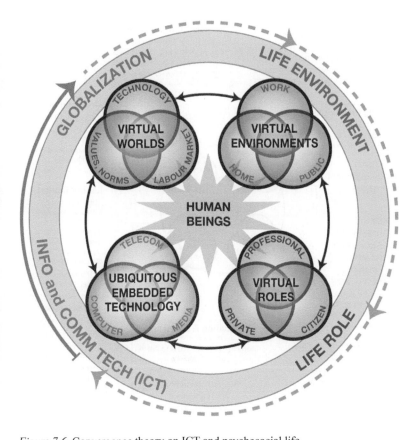

Figure 7.6 Convergence theory on ICT and psychosocial life

was dropped in this book title, as being too long a title, but it appears with a "T" in "ICT". The actions are also related to the convergence theory, which is strengthening the reasoning that lies behind these societal changes. To illustrate this connection and logic, I return now to the presentation of the theory which first took place in Chapter 3, and thereby use the same graphics *within* these three Figures, 7.5. 7.6, and 7.7. I can say that these three figures constitute, together with the manifesto, a summary of the entire book.

Figure 7.5 is a reminder of the phenomenon of convergence – the basis for my theory. Convergence leads forward to a new colour, new shades, and new forms, which mean new risks and opportunities for people and society. Convergence is unforeseeable. As to technology, we can observe more and more convergences between nanotech, biotech, artificial intelligence (AI), web, Internet,

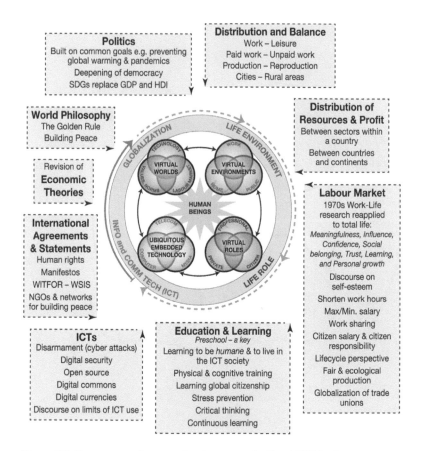

Figure 7.7 Convergence theory and actions toward a Good ICT Society

Note: SDGs = Sustainable Development Goals; GDP = Gross Domestic Product; HDI = The Human Development Index

and media that have consequences for various realms of life. Figure 7.5 was presented already in theory in Chapter 3. Coloured figures in the e-book version of this book facilitate the connection between the three figures; however, when converting figure 7.5 to black-and-white for the hardcover book, the middle part of the model, where the three dimensional subparts converge, appears on a kind of molecule level. Each little molecule is dancing with the others: this illustrates how a new unknown sphere is being shaped in depth.

Figure 7.6 illustrates my convergence theory with its sub parts. It is presented already in Chapter 3 about theory. However here, in Chapter 7, which deals with actions to achieve the Good ICT Society, I want to show how actions could be related to and derived from the theory (Figure 7.7).

Figure 7.7 describes actions to achieve the Good ICT Society. The actions are related to the convergence theory, but they are also structured in the same way as my manifesto. Each box among the 10 boxes corresponds to one of the 10 top actions. This is my way of summarizing a little book that got as its title, "The Good ICT Society – From Theory to Actions". For some time beforehand, it was instead entitled, "In Search of Wisdom in the ICT Society".

Dear Reader, I invite you to write to me and contribute with your wisdom and your own experiences to what you think are the main changes and what actions you think are most important for co-creating the Good ICT Society. You can comment on any of the circles or clusters in Figure 7.6 or any of the action boxes in Figure 7.7. Let us together grow wisdom and love in the ICT society! Please write to me at gbradley[at]kth.se.

ICT is a beautiful technology, a way to "extend the Good" and "magnify the Good" and to focus on a global humane morality/ethics. There is *a high potential for the good society for all – an embryo for democracy, well-being, health, and quality of life for all*. Visions, awareness, and actions are urgently needed due to the speed and power connected to these ever-converging and constantly emerging technologies. A tool box as the one in 7.7 is one roadmap for actions. Let us together stop any trial of misuse. Bottom up and top down.

Bibliography

Bates, T. (2015). *Teaching in the Digital Age: Guidelines for Designing*. Victoria, BC: BC Campus.

Bradley, G. (1989). *Computers and the Psychosocial Work Environment*. London/ Philadelphia, UK/PA: Taylor & Francis.

Convivialist Manifesto. A Declaration of Interdependence: With An Introduction by Frank Adloff. Translated from the French by Margaret Clarke. Global Dialogues 3, Duisburg 2014. www.gcr21.org/publications/global-dialogues/2198-0403-gd-3/

eEurope – An Information Society for All. www.euractiv.com/section/digital/ linksdossier/eeurope-an-information-society-for-all/

The European Citizens' Initiative (ECI) Is a European Union Mechanism Aimed at Increasing Direct Democracy by Enabling the EU Citizens to Participate Directly in the Development of EU Policies, Introduced with the Treaty of Lisbon in 2007. https://en.wikipedia.org/wiki/European_Citizens%27_Initiative.

Floridi, L. (ed.). (2015). *The Onlife Manifesto – Being Human in a Hyperconnected Era*. Springer Open. *The Manifesto* was the outcome of the work of a group of scholars, organized by DG Connect within the European Commission. As chair was Luciano Floridi (Other participants were: Stefana Broadbent, Nicole Dewandre, Charles Ess, Jean-Gabriel Ganascia, Mireille Hildebrandt, Yiannis Laouris, Claire Lobet-Maris, Sarah Oates, Ugo Pagallo, Judith Simon, May Thorseth, and Peter-Paul Verbeek).

Patrignani, N. and Whitehouse, D. (2014). Slow Tech: The Bridge between Computer Ethics and Business Ethics. *ICT and Society Volume 431 of the Series IFIP Advances in Information and Communication Technology*, 92–106.

Patrignani, N. and Whitehouse, D. (2017). *Slow Tech – Steps Towards a Good, Clean, and Fair Information and Communication Technology*. London: Palgrave Macmillan.

Schuler, D. (2016). *Civic Intelligence* – a Type of Collective Intelligence That Addresses Substantial Shared Problems Both Effectively and Fairly: Intelligence, Whether in a Single Person or Collectively, in Classes, Cities, Nations or the World, Is Seen as a Complex Ecosystem and Not Just in the Head, but Deeply Entangled with Action, Including Planning, Evaluating, Doing and Interacting with Other People (Civic Intelligence Laboratory at Evergreen State College in Washington).

Selg, H. (2014). *Researching the Use of the Internet – A Beginner's Guide*. Uppsala Dissertations from the Faculty of Science and Technology, University dissertation from the Faculty of Science and Technology, Uppsala: Acta Universitatis Upsaliensis.

Strassburger, V.C., Jordan A.B., and Donnerstein, E. (2010). Health Effects of Media on Children and Adolescents (Review Article). *Pediatrics*, April, 125, 756–767.

The Transforming Power of Digitalization – from Words to Action (Swedish title: *Digitaliseringens tranformerande kraft – från ord till handling*). (2015). Official Reports of the Swedish Government (SOU 2015:91).

Victorin, Å. Course Material for School and Preschool Children That Gives Guidance to Parents and Teachers in Order to Prevent Unhealthy Habits and Promote a Great and Happy Childhood. www.qleva.se.

Acknowledgements

When starting to write on a new book or report I often used to make a drawing of a bunch of balloons that I filled with various colours. They represented chapter contents and got preliminary titles. Over the years some balloons disappeared and/or merged with other balloons and some left the bunch, like seeds that did not receive soil enough to grow. Some needed more reflection, more oxygen to be able to keep the string upwards.

Many persons have been involved in my book journey and there are some I particularly would like to bring my thanks.

To Diane Whitehouse, one of the driving souls within IFIP. We worked together on mainly two chapters, Chapter 4, "Towards peace on earth", and Chapter 5, "Voices from around the world on quality of life and well-being in the ICT society". Diane has inspired me during the process of the book writing, and we had several meetings when we both discussed the book and prepared panels and program for the IADIS conference "ICT, Society, and Human Beings" that we co-chaired for some years. There were moments that were at the top of creativity and fun.

Naomi Lubick, science writer from California, came into my world in the spring 2016 and contributed substantially to the book with her knowledge and encouragement. She gave me a sincere self-confidence at a time when I was ready to interrupt the book project. She made me recognize the strengths in my text through short notes and "hurrahs".

To Cajsa Tengblad, author and lecturer in family health, a woman I met at a course entitled "Writing your life". She took a weekend out from her family and read a draft of the manuscript and concluded that she would like to see more of me, Gunilla, my thinking, reflections, and conclusions, in the book.

My very good friend Geraldine Hultkrantz is a permanent supporter at my writings, my preparations of key note speeches, and my initiatives. This is built on a long friendship including our roles as grandmothers.

Darek Haftor, professor and leader of the "Gunilla Bradley Research Center of Digital Business" at Linnaeus University in Sweden, thank you for seeing positive alternatives at crossroads and encouragement.

Miranda Kajtazi, lecturer at Lund University, thank you for very kindly taking time to read the manuscript on a flight across the Atlantic heading to Canada.

I am grateful to all interviewed persons, who so generously contributed with their thoughts and experiences.

Coming closer to the final date I asked members of my extended family to review certain chapters. Thanks for valuable comments to Karin Bradley, associate professor at Royal Institute of Technology, and Linda Bradley, director of Diamond Experts on International Expansion.

Special thanks to the great people at Routledge and also to the anonymous reviewers.

Bibliography

Ackoff, R. L. (1989). From Data to Wisdom. *Journal of Applied Systems Analysis*, 16, 3–9.

Asimov, I. (1942). *Runaround*. Astounding Science Fiction, March, 1942.

Asimov, I. The Robot Novels: *I, Robot*, (1950) ISBN 0-553-29438-5; *The Rest of the Robots*, (1964) ISBN 0-385-09041-2; *Robot Dreams*, (1986) ISBN 0-441-73154-6.

Ball, K. and Webster, F. (eds.). (2003). *The Intensification of Surveillance: Crime, Terrorism and Warfare in the Information Era*. London: Pluto Press.

Bates, T. (2015). *Teaching in the Digital Age: Guidelines for Designing*. Victoria, BC: BC Campus.

Berleur, J., Beardon, C. and Laufer, R. (eds.). (1993). Facing the Challenge of Risk and Vulnerability in an Information Society. Proceedings of the IFIP WG9.2 Working Conference on Facing the Challenge of Risk and Vulnerability in an Information Society, Namur, Belgium, 20–22 May.

Bjurner, A. and Wallensteen, P. (2014). *Regional Organizations in Peacemaking: Challengers to the UN?* London: Routledge.

boyd, d. (2015). *It's Complicated: The Social Lives of Networked Teens*. New Haven, CT: Yale University Press.

Bradley, G. (1977). *Datateknik, arbetsliv och kommunikation. (Computer Technology, Work Life, and Communication)*. The Swedish delegation for long term research. FRN. Liber (in Swedish), Stockholm, SE.

Bradley, G. (1979). Professional Roles and Life Environment (Swedish title: *Yrkesroller och Livsmiljö*). Stockholm, SE: Wahlström, & Widstrand. ISBN: 91-46-13409-3.

Bradley, G. (1989). *Computers and the Psychosocial Work Environment*. London/ Philadelphia, UK/PA: Taylor & Francis.

Bradley, G. (ed.). (2001). *Humans on the Net: Information and Communication Technology (ICT) Work Organization and Human Beings*. Stockholm, SE: Prevent. ISBN 91-7522-701-0.

Bradley, G. (2006). *Social and Community Informatics – Humans on the Net*. London/ New York: Routledge.

Bradley, G. (ed.) (2008). Book of Proceedings of the IADIS International Conference: ICT Society and Human Beings, within MCCSIS (Multi-Conference on Computer Science and Information Systems). Amsterdam, The Netherlands, July 22–24, 2008. IADIS Press.

Bradley, G. (2010). Special Invited Chapter on The Convergence Theory on ICT, Society and Human Beings – towards the Good ICT Society. In: Haftor, D. and Mirijamdotter, A. (eds.), *Information and Communication Technologies, Society and Human Beings – Festschrift in Honor of Gunilla Bradley*. New York: IGI Global, 30–46. ISBN: 978-1-60960-057-0.

Bradley, G. (2011). The Convergence Theory on ICT, Society and Human Beings: Towards the Good ICT Society. In: Haftor, D. and Mirijamdotter, A. (eds.), *Information and Communication Technologies, Society and Human Beings*. New York: IGI Global, 30–46.

Bradley, G. (2014). Social Informatics and Ethics: Towards the Good Information and Communication Society. In: Fuchs, C. and Sandoval, M. (eds.), *Critique, Social Media and the Information Society*. London/New York: Routledge, 91–105.

Bradley, G. (2015). TED Talk by Gunilla Bradley on *Change of Habits in the ICT Society*. http://tedxtalks.ted.com/video/Understanding-the-Change-of-Hab. *A TED seminar was held* in November 2014 in the city of Växjö at the Linnaeus University in Sweden, organized by Dr Miranda Kajtazi.

Bradley, G. (2016). In Search of Wisdom in the ICT Society – Theory and Visions. In: Burgin, M. and Hofkirchner, W. (eds.), *The Future Information Society: Social and Technological Problems*. World Scientific, 123–136.

Bradley, G., Whitehouse, D., Singh, G. (eds.) (2011). Book of Proceedings of the IADIS International Conferences: ICT, Society and Human Beings, and eDemocracy, Equity and Social Justice, within MCCSIS. Rome, Italy, July 20–26, 2011. IADIS Press.

Bradley, G., Whitehouse, D., and Lin (eds.) (2012). Book of Proceedings of the IADIS International Conferences: ICT, Society and Human Beings, and eCommerce, within MCCSIS. Lisbon, Portugal, July 17–23, 2012. IADIS Press.

Bradley, K. (2014). Towards a peer economy – How open source and peer-to-peer architecture, hardware and consumption are transforming the economy. In Bradley, K. & Hedrén, J. (eds.), Green utopianism – Perspectives, politics and micro-practices. New York: Routledge.

Bradley, L. and Bradley, G. (2000). Home of the Future and ICT – Integration of Professional and Private Roles. Special Issue of "Ergonomics", Vol. 43, No. 6 and Included in the Congress CD-ROM Proceedings at the IEA/HFES 2000 Congress, San Diego, USA, Taylor & Francis, London.

Bradley, L. and Bradley, G. (2001). The Home as a Virtual and Physical Space – Experiences from USA and South-East Asia. In: Smith, M. J. and Salvendy, G. (eds.), *Systems, Social and Internationalization Design Aspects of Human – Computer Interaction*. Mahwah, NJ: Lawrence Erlbaum Ass. Inc., 81–85.

Cameron, J. (2011). A Survival Kit for Resilient Citizens in the Information Society. Presentation Made at the IFIP WG9.2 & WG 9.9 Joint Workshop, Milan, Social Accountability & Sustainability in the Information Society: Perspectives on Long-Term Responsibility, 4–5 June 2011.

Castells, M. (2000). Trilogy on *The Information Age. Economy, Society and Culture*. Daidalos Publisher.

Castells, M. (2001). *The Internet galaxy*. Oxford, UK: Oxford University Press.

Convivialist Manifesto. A Declaration of Interdependence: With An Introduction by Frank Adloff. Translated from the French by Margaret Clarke. Global Dialogues 3, Duisburg 2014. www.gcr21.org/publications/global-dialogues/2198-0403-gd-3/

Danielsson, U. (2007). *Relationships between Information Communication Technology and Psychosocial Life Environment: Students and Young Urban Knowledge Workers in the ICT-Era*. Doctoral dissertation at Department of Informatics, Mid Sweden University.

Davis, F. D., Bagozzi, R. P., & Warshaw, P. R. (1989). User acceptance of computer technology: A comparison of two theoretical models. *Management Science*, 35(8), 983–1003.

Doyle, M.W. and Sambrinis, N. (2006). *Making War and Building Peace: United Nations Peace Operations*. Princeton, NJ: Princeton University Press.

Economist, The. (2010). The War in the Fifth Domain: Are the Mouse and the Keyboard the New Weapons of Conflict? July 1 2010. www.economist.com/node/16478792, accessed 19 July 2014.

eEurope – An Information Society for All. www.euractiv.com/section/digital/linksdossier/eeurope-an-information-society-for-all/

ETHICOMP. (2013). The Possibilities of Ethical ICT. University of Southern Denmark, Kolding, Denmark, 12 June–14 June 2013.

The European Citizens' Initiative (ECI) Is a European Union Mechanism Aimed at Increasing Direct Democracy by Enabling the EU Citizens to Participate Directly in the Development of EU Policies, Introduced with the Treaty of Lisbon in 2007. https://en.wikipedia.org/wiki/European_Citizens%27_Initiative.

European Commission. (2012). *Tackling Crime in Our Digital Age: Establishing a European Cybercrime Centre*. Brussels: European Commission. 28.03.2012. COM (2012) 140 Final. http://ec.europa.eu/home-affairs/doc_centre/crime/docs/Communication%20-%20European%20Cybercrime%20Centre.pdf, accessed 19 July 2014.

Ewerman, A. (1996). *Marknaden 1000 År – Fem eror i Europa* (*The Market 1000 Years – Five Eras in Europe*). Stockholm: Ewerman Business Intelligence AB.

Floridi, L. (ed.). (2015). *The Onlife Manifesto – Being Human in a Hyperconnected Era*. Springer Open. *The Manifesto* was the outcome of the work of a group of scholars, organized by DG Connect within the European Commission. As chair was Luciano Floridi (Other participants were: Stefana Broadbent, Nicole Dewandre, Charles Ess, Jean-Gabriel Ganascia, Mireille Hildebrandt, Yiannis Laouris, Claire Lobet-Maris, Sarah Oates, Ugo Pagallo, Judith Simon, May Thorseth, and Peter-Paul Verbeek).

Gardner, H. and Davis, K. (2014). *The App Generation: How Today's Youth Navigate Identity, Intimacy, and Imagination in a Digital World*. New Haven, CT: Yale University Press.

Giddens, A. (1990). *The consequences of modernity.* Cambridge, UK: Polity.

Giddens, A. (2000). *Runaway world.* London, UK: Routledge.

Habermas, J. (1989). *The structural transformation of the public sphere.* Cambridge, UK: Polity.

Höglund, K. and Fjelde, H. (eds). (2011). *Building Peace, Creating Conflict: Conflictual Dimensions of Local and International Peacebuilding*. Lund, Sweden: Nordic Academic Press.

https://en.oxforddictionaries.com/definition/wisdom

https://en.wikipedia.org/wiki/Wisdom#Definitions

Inglehart and Welzel (2015). The International Value Map. Recreation of the 2010 map. https://en.wikipedia.org/wiki/Inglehart%E2%80%93Welzel_cultural_map_of_the_world https://en.wikipedia.org/wiki/Human_Development_Index

Jensen, R. (1999). *The dream society*. New York/London, NY/UK: McGraw-Hill.

Kajtazi, M. (2012). An Exploration of Information Inadequacy: The Lack of Needed Information in Human, Social and Industrial Affairs. In: Hercheui, M., Whitehouse, D., Phahlamohlaka, and McIver, W.J., Jr (eds.), *ICT Critical Infrastructures and Society: IFIP Advances in Information and Communication Technology*. Berlin/Heidelberg, Germany: Springer-Verlag.

Kavathatzopoulos, I. (2014). Independent Agents and Ethics. In: Kimppa, K., Whitehouse, D., Kuusela, T., and Phahlamohlaka, J. (eds.), *ICT and Society: Advances in Information and Communication Technology*. Berlin/Heidelberg: Springer, 39–46.

Khakhar, D. (ed.). (2003). *WITFOR 2003 White Book, Proceedings of IFIP World Information Technology Forum*. Laxenburg, Austria: IFIP Press.

Konrath, S. H., O'Brien, E. H. and Hsing, C. (2011). Changes in Dispositional Empathy in American College Students Over Time: A Meta-Analysis. *Personality and Social Psychology*, 15 (2), 80–198.

Kuhn, T. S. (1962). *The Structure of Scientific Revolutions*. Chicago: University of Chicago Press.

Lepore, J. (2016). Review of the Book by Michael Lynch. *The New Yorker*, March 21 2016.

Lindgren, M., Furth, T. and Luhti, B. (2005). *The MeWe Generation*. Stockholm: Bookhouse Publishing.

Livingstone, S. (2014). In Their Own Words: What Bothers Children Online? *European Journal of Communication*, June, 29, 271–288, first published on March 3, 2014.

Livingstone, S., Haddon, L., Görzig, A. and Ólafsson, K. (2011). *Risks and Safety on the Internet: The Perspective of European Children: Full Findings and Policy Implications from the EU Kids Online Survey of 9–16 Year Olds and Their Parents in 25 Countries*. London, UK: EU Kids Online, Deliverable D4. EU Kids Online Network.

Lynch, M. P. (2016). *The Internet of Us: Knowing More and Understanding Less in the Age of Big Data*. New York: W.W. Norton.

Melville, N., Kraemer, K., & Gurbaxani, V. (2004). Information technology and organisational performance: An integrative model of IT business value. *MIS Quarterly*, 45(2), 283–322.

Olsson, A., Petrovic, P. and Ingvar, M. (2012). *Så ska EU stoppa cyberbrotten*. DN Debate.

Orito, Y. and Murata, K. (2014). Dividualisation: Objectified and Partialised Human Beings. Conference paper, CEPE 2014.

Patrignani, N. and Whitehouse, D. (2014). Slow Tech: The Bridge between Computer Ethics and Business Ethics. *ICT and Society Volume 431 of the Series IFIP Advances in Information and Communication Technology*, 92–106.

Patrignani, N. and Whitehouse, D. (2017). *Slow Tech – Steps Towards a Good, Clean, and Fair Information and Communication Technology*. London: Palgrave Macmillan.

Schiller, H. (1993). Public way of private road? *The Nation*, 12, 64–66.

Schuler, D. (2016). *Civic Intelligence* – a Type of Collective Intelligence That Addresses Substantial Shared Problems Both Effectively and Fairly: Intelligence, Whether in a Single Person or Collectively, in Classes, Cities, Nations or the World, Is Seen as a Complex Ecosystem and Not Just in the Head, but Deeply Entangled with Action, Including Planning, Evaluating, Doing and Interacting with Other People (Civic Intelligence Laboratory at Evergreen State College in Washington).

Schultz, W. (1994). *The Human Element.* San Francisco: Jossey-Bass Publishers.

Schultze, U. & Orlikowski, W. J. (2001). Metaphors of virtuality: shaping an emergent reality. In *Information and Organization*, 45–77.

Selg, H. (2014). *Researching the Use of the Internet – A Beginner's Guide.* Uppsala Dissertations from the Faculty of Science and Technology, University dissertation from the Faculty of Science and Technology, Uppsala: Acta Universitatis Upsaliensis.

Strassburger, V.C., Jordan A.B., and Donnerstein, E. (2010). Health Effects of Media on Children and Adolescents (Review Article). *Pediatrics*, April, 125, 756–767.

The Sustainable Development Goals (SDGs), Officially Known as Transforming Our World: The 2030 Agenda for Sustainable Development. www.un.org/sustainable development/sustainable-development-goals/

SvD Opinion. (2012). Så ska EU stoppa cyberbrotten. 28 March 2012. www.svd. se/opinion/brannpunkt/sa-ska-eu-stoppa-cyberbrotten_6957681.svd, accessed 19 July 2014.

Swedish Media Council. (2011). *The Violent Computer Games and Aggression – an Overview of the Research 2000–2011.* Swedish Media Council. www.statensme dierad.se, accessed 19 July 2014.

Swingle, M. (2006). *I-Minds: How Cell Phones, Computers, Gaming, and Social Media are Changing Our Brains, Our Behavior, and the Evolution of Our Species.* British Columbia: New Society Publishers.

The Transforming Power of Digitalization – from Words to Action (Swedish title: *Digitaliseringens tranformerande kraft – från ord till handling*). (2015). Official Reports of the Swedish Government (SOU 2015:91).

Touré, H.I. (2011). *The Quest for Cyber Peace.* Geneva, Switzerland: International Telecommunications Union.

UCDP (The Uppsala Conflict Data Program) offers a number of datasets on organized violence and peacemaking, most of which are updated on an annual basis. http://ucdp. uu.se or directly http://ucdp.uu.se/downloads. The UCDP Conflict Encyclopedia (UCDP database) is an online, free of charge, database containing detailed descriptive information on armed conflicts, peace agreements, and several other aspects of organized violence. Coverage is global with information from 1946 and onwards.

Universal Declaration of Human Rights – the United Nations. www.un.org/en/ udhrbook/pdf/udhr_booklet_en_web.pdf

Uppsala Center for Peace Research Info. www.pcr.uu.se/about/news_archive/2015, accessed 31 December 2015.

Van der Heijden. (2004). User acceptance of hedonic Information Systems. *MIS Quarterly* 28(4), 695–704.

Victorin, Å. Course Material for School and Preschool Children That Gives Guidance to Parents and Teachers in Order to Prevent Unhealthy Habits and Promote a Great and Happy Childhood. www.qleva.se.

Wallensteen, P. (2015). *Quality Peace: Peacebuilding, Victory and World Order.* Oxford: Oxford University Press.

Walsham, G. (2005). Development, global futures and IS research: a polemic. In *Journal of Strategic Information Systems,* 14, 5–15.

Webster, F. (1995). *Theories of the Information Society.* London: Routledge.

Whitehouse, D. (2012). Benchmarking eHealth in the European Union. Presentation Made at the IFIP WG9.2 Workshop on, ICT Critical Infrastructure and Social Accountability: Methods, Tools and Techniques. London, 4 February 2012.

Whitehouse, D., Hilty, L., Patrignani, N. and Lieshout, M. van. (2011). Introduction. In: Whitehouse, D., Hilty, L., Patrignani, N., and Lieshout, M. van (eds.), *Social Accountability and Sustainability in the Information Society: Perspectives in Long-Term Responsibility.* Rome: Notizie di Politeia, 3–12.

WITFOR World IT Forum: Vilnius Declaration 2003, p. 2; see also Khakhar (2003).

Zaki J., and Ochsner, K. (2012). The neuroscience of empathy: progress, pitfalls and promise. *Nature Neuroscience* 15, 675–680.

Zartmann, W. (2004). Pronouncement at Event Entitled Civil War: Need, Creed and Greed. October 21, 2004. www.cgdev.org/content/calendar/detail/3019/, accessed 19 July 2014.

Index

For Product Safety Concerns and Information please contact our
EU representative GPSR@taylorandfrancis.com Taylor & Francis
Verlag GmbH, Kaufingerstraße 24, 80331 München, Germany